ALWAYS

SQUEEZING

LEMONS

Taking Responsibility to
Define Your Own Success

KAYLA LOGUE

ALWAYS SQUEEZING LEMONS
BY KAYLA LOGUE
©2024 Kayla Logue

Print ISBN - 979-8-35094-774-8
eBook ISBN - 979-8-35094-775-5

https://www.kaylalogue.com/

First edition.

Dedicated to everyone who has loved, helped, and believed in me along the way. Your support has never gone unnoticed and will never be forgotten.

XOXO

CONTENTS

INTRODUCTION

On a scorching summer day, would you skip adding ice to your freshly squeezed lemonade?

If you say yes, you're lying. Or, you live in the Arctic and don't need to add ice to anything. The ice is the key; it's the thirst-quenching element. Yes, you need the lemonade, but without the ice, is it as satisfying?

In a book, the introduction is the ice, and the rest of the chapters are the steps needed to make a tall, delicious glass of lemonade. You can skip reading it, but you won't fully quench your thirst. You need ice to be satisfied.

So, do not skip the introduction, because you need to read it to understand how this book will help you.

That's the only way you will be completely satisfied with this book.

So, let's break the ice and take our first, thirst-quenching sip.

SUCCESS STARTS WITH YOU

It was 3:20 AM on a Wednesday in late July of 2020 when I woke up, grabbed my phone, and typed out the first real ideas for the book I had always wanted to write in my notes app. It had been almost four months since I left my eight-year relationship and three-year marriage, my loving dog, a thriving Pilates career, and decided to blow up my "perfect" life.

I was staying with one of my closest friends on St. Simons Island, Georgia. I slept in bed with her that night, and I can still vividly remember being wide awake and the weird clarity that came to me while I typed, lying there, until the sun came up.

My mind was racing, and I had to get my thoughts written down.

It had been a restless night—I had been thinking a lot about how I was feeling regarding my decision to leave, and I was finally able to start expressing those thoughts. Chills ran up and down my spine as thoughts and feelings seamlessly flowed into words in my notes. It was the first time I could see my unhinged words written down—I could also feel the connection between my words and the message I knew I wanted to continue to unfold and deliver.

I wanted to share what I was feeling on a large scale. I wanted to share my story in the pages of a book.

This energy and clarity came from the faith I had in myself that I could overcome anything, that it all started and ended with me, and that I would be always squeezing lemons.

I realized that no matter how much bullshit life had, I could always squeeze lemons to make lemonade. I was responsible for my actions and responses to make the most of whatever came my way. I made a conscious decision to remove negativity and move forward, prioritizing positivity.

I realized I could be the cause, problem, and solution for everything in my life, and my world changed. I am in control of my success, however I choose to define that, as well as my habits, thoughts, words, and actions.

Through this awareness, I recognized that by squeezing the lemons of my life, I was serving something greater.

When I had the idea to write *Always Squeezing Lemons*, I didn't know what it would look like at the end. Now, I know it was to give back to others by sharing my experience, the knowledge I've gained, and the help I've been given by the loving and supportive people I've gathered around me throughout it all.

I learned to love, forgive, and admire myself in order to be able to do the same for others. And I captured it all in the pages of my journals.

Now you're reading the edited versions of those early-morning musings in the pages of this book, *Always Squeezing Lemons*.

But let me back up a minute and give you a little more context.

In May 2020, when I was twenty-five, everything in my life changed. I was a Pilates instructor with a rigorous health and fitness routine, married, and living in Alexandria, Virginia. It was what many would consider a "picture-perfect" life, but I decided the life I had built with my now ex-husband wasn't the right life for me. So, with $900 in my pocket, I left that life behind. My goals, what I wanted to accomplish, and my definition of success had changed. This book is about that journey.

Success is subjective. We can define it individually because there isn't one title or achievement that encompasses it. As we change, so do our goals, accomplishments, and measurements of success. What is *not* changeable are the principles to achieve success, which always start with you.

If we want something greater for ourselves, however we define it, we must learn to overcome the obstacles and challenges that come with failure, hurt, and heartbreak.

Leaving a marriage and an entire life I had worked so hard to build could have been considered a failure. It was heartbreaking to leave that life—friends, colleagues, my dog, and even the man I had spent eight years with.

I felt suffocated. I knew I was capped out, and I was trying to be happy in a life that did not fit. I knew nothing would change unless I decided to do so. When I committed to moving on, it seemed sudden to everyone else, but for me, it had been building for years.

No one understood the depths of it, and I did not expect them to. I had support from family and close friends, and I was confident in myself and my decision—I felt freer than ever when I decided to move on. I can still feel the release I experienced when I finally committed to that decision.

I did not dwell on this, though, and have since spent my time cultivating resilience. With my new mindset adopted, I turned what would typically be seen (and even felt) as negative into a positive learning experience. I do not view pain, inconveniences, or failure as roadblocks, only speedbumps.

I keep going.

I've built a résumé of overcoming obstacles, and in turn, have built confidence knowing everything happens for a reason, and no matter what, I always have control over my responses. Like success, failure can be subjective. I do not focus on anyone else's definition and stay true to my internal reference point.

We have to learn to become resilient and mentally strong enough to recognize the only control we ever have in any situation is our response.

What typically holds us back from mental resilience? Fear. Human nature seeks validation and recognition. It's why we are hyper-focused on big wins but crumble at a loss.

We are scared of failure and judgment.

We are scared of change and discomfort.

We are scared of uncertainty.

We are scared of being alone.

We are scared of rejection.

We are scared of disappointment.

And we are scared of being imperfect.

For a long time, I was constantly scared of judgment and disappointment. That's why I pursued a "picture-perfect," status-quo life. I'm *still* a little scared of judgment and disappointment—I haven't completely overcome these fears.

Writing this book brought up a lot of that fear: I hate to disappoint anyone I love and will sometimes compromise myself and my boundaries to make them happy. But what is different now is that I am aware of it. I know my response is in my control. I also know we are all experts in our own experience. We are all the same, but none of us live or experience life the same way. I've found a lot of confidence in this idea, and it has helped me overcome my greatest fears, rooted in things I have no control over.

(Except for my fear of toads. I hate the way they move; they are disgustingly huge to be able to hop that way. I legit lose my mind whenever I see a toad, and I don't think I'm overcoming that fear anytime soon.)

We define our success, and it starts with facing these fears. It's the only way to be unapologetically you.

SETBACK? COMEBACK.

This is not a how-to book about success. It is about the learning experiences, failures, mistakes, hurt, and heartbreak that inspired my resilience and mental grit. Mental grit includes passion and perseverance—a person with mental grit has the qualities to persevere and succeed in the face of adversity.

I have failed, I have experienced heartbreak, and I have learned a lot. I left my "perfect life" with less than $1,000 to my name.

I had no direction, but I did have mental grit.

And that led to my new definition of success. Less than three years later, I won the Top Sales Producer award for one of the largest land development companies in the country and have earned over seven figures in pure commissions—all before thirty. I became successful, but I don't define it with what I accomplished financially—I define it by the strengths I was able to identify and capitalize on. With several other small and major wins—and a lot of mistakes, pain, and resilience in between—this book is about my wild journey, the lessons I learned, and how I turned a setback into a comeback.

Because I was stuck. My "perfect life" was only serving the life I *thought* I was supposed to live. The one that checked all the boxes.

But it wasn't the life *I* wanted to live. I was scared for many reasons...until I wasn't. (The fears did not go away—they're all still there—but I've taken control of them.)

No matter how big or small the situation, we are typically holding back on ourselves out of fear of failure.

My fear of failure used to be based on validation, judgment, and someone else's definition of success. Fear paralyzed me.

I still have a fear of failure, but it has evolved. I am now terrified if I do *not* hold myself accountable to my own goals, promises, and actions to better serve myself and others around me. I'm terrified to make false promises to myself that prohibit me from showing up as the best version of myself. I still feel fear often, but I now have experienced and understand faith and courage conquer fear. Fear no longer paralyzes me.

We're terrified to make a mistake because we don't want to get hurt or experience heartbreak; we don't want to lose out on what we had.

When one door closes, another opens. Your setback gears you up for your next comeback.

How do we embrace our setbacks, so we're geared up for the next comeback?

We have to actually start. We have to take the first step.

If I hadn't, I would still be living a life I didn't love. And I certainly wouldn't have been able to leap into a new career or form the new relationships I have. And I for damn sure would not have written this book.

Only you can take your first step...but I can help.

In the upcoming chapters, I will tell you a little about my personal journey. I will also tell you the mistakes I made, and the lessons learned along the way. I will share my experiences with heavy topics that required a lot of honesty and vulnerability from me. I hope my stories can be of value to you in your life.

Each chapter will be a step in the process of turning a lemon into lemonade—I do not have an obsession with lemons...but I do with metaphors. I wasn't able to squeeze the lemons of my life into lemonade right away; it was a step-by-step process.

Also, while you're reading, pay special attention to the dates. You will quickly understand that my journey has been quite a roller coaster and is pieced together through experiences with time stamps. Growth will never be a linear journey, but my growth journey is a damn good one.

Each chapter will also include a Lemon Drop, a recap of the chapter's lesson, for quick and easy reference, and a journal prompt. As you'll come to learn in Chapter 3, journaling was one of the activities that helped me heal and grow the most. I want to share that practice with you.

Throughout this book, you'll see how important journaling has been for me. It has been my therapy—every story and break-through I share was rooted, emotionally refined, or mani-fested through journaling. It allowed me to establish a level of self-awareness I never had before.

I want this for every single one of you, which is why I included a journal prompt at the end of each chapter. Feel free to use them, or not—it is ultimately up to you. If you already practice journaling, I know you appreciate a good prompt when it is in front of you—I hope you find help with mine. If journaling is new to you, I challenge you to use the prompts to kick-start your journaling journey.

TAKE RESPONSIBILITY: YOU HAVE ALL THE ANSWERS

I am living a life I genuinely love...but I wasn't always. I wrote this book to share how I've grown and continue to evolve.

And I want to help you do the same, so you can live a life you love, too.

My journey has been (and continues to be) a healing process—I am more self-aware and can now face my fears *and* embrace my failures. I confidently understand how my purpose continues to evolve, know my strengths, and trust myself to make the best possible decision in the moment.

Making mistakes, judgment or disappointment are no longer fears of mine. Through this work, I redefined my values and trusted myself wholeheartedly to figure it out and make it happen. I did a lot of self-reflection to understand who I was, what I wanted, and how to love myself.

And then I acted upon it.

I did not make excuses; I took full responsibility for everything I did—I did not let fear hold me back. I had a plan for every decision I made. I had systems and goals in place to succeed, but I was also prepared for failure. I was not afraid of rejection and said no when I needed to.

I never back down from challenges; in fact, I seek them, and I learned to thrive in the uncomfortable state of change. I never threw a pity party for myself (don't worry, I vented *a lot*), but I instead used the hurt and pain I experienced as motivation to keep going to find and love myself again. I figured out how to thrive in evolving environments.

During all of this, I am still a mess sometimes. I have full mental breakdowns when I feel like I completely suck at everything in life. These days, I want to sit on my couch and blast sad, sappy love songs while I cry my eyes out with a bottle of wine.

The obvious truth is that gets me nowhere.

We all need a deep cry every once in a while—we have to give ourselves some grace—but ultimately, the root solution to the tears is not in love songs or at the bottom of that bottle of wine.

The answers are only to be found within you and *by* you.

I can make a tall, thirst-quenching glass of lemonade. But I had to squeeze a lot of lemons to get here.

SMILE FOR THE CAMERA

*"The greatest act of self-love is to no longer accept
a life you are unhappy with."*

—BRIANNA WIEST, *THE MOUNTAIN IS YOU*

. . . .

Lemonade. It has always been a signature summertime beverage. Cold, sweet, and tart, and absolutely thirst-quenching.

It is delicious.

When life gives us lemons, we're supposed to make lemonade, yes?

The first step is to decide to turn those lemons into lemonade in the first place.

. . . .

JULY 24, 2020

Before publishing *Always Squeezing Lemons*, I had thought about writing a book for a long time. I honestly do not know when I first realized it was something I *definitely* wanted to do, but I *do* remember the first time I wrote something down, when the concept no longer lived in my thoughts.

Remember that night I mentioned a few pages ago when I first realized what this book was going to be about? That was when I first started journaling, was working on self-development, and had absolutely no clue what my next move was going to be in any area of my life, yet I felt an incredibly positive pull toward the vision of writing a book. For most people in my current circumstances, I knew the decision to do so would make no sense, but for me, there was an energy that developed that I was not going to let die.

Over the next two-and-a-half years, I filled journal pages and phone notes with a lot of feelings, thoughts, visions, and details of the way my chaotic life was unfolding. I had an ardent desire to grow by sharing more. I wanted to give back by sharing my experience, knowledge, service, help, love, and support for others in an admirable way. I found the confidence to be able to express myself through writing. I felt like I took control when I put pen to paper.

A "PICTURE-PERFECT" LIFE?

What may look and seem perfect to someone else is not necessarily what is right and perfect for you. The life they're meant to live isn't the life you're meant to live.

When I found myself at my lowest mental point, no one would have known. I lived what looked like the most ideal life—the "picture perfect" one we all strive for. I was married to a very handsome, intelligent man who was always the life of the party. In social settings, we were the people you wanted to be around. We could make friends with anyone, anywhere, and at any time of the day.

I met my ex-husband in college, at the University of South Carolina, in Beaufort. He was a baseball player—a fifth-year senior—and I played softball my freshman year. We had the best rescue pup ever, Jemma, whom we adopted together when we were there.

My ex and I lived in Old Town, Alexandria. A beautiful, historical town in Virginia right outside of DC. It is a highly sought-out place to live with literally anything and everything anyone would want to do, all within the town limits. I managed a boutique Pilates studio, Solidcore, within a five-minute walk from our charming townhome. I made my own schedule, worked out a lot, and as a fitness coach in a remarkably high-stress area, I was probably the best part of a lot of people's days. With my flexible schedule, I was able to spend a lot of time working on our patio while Jemma chased squirrels all day in the backyard.

We spent every weekend in Harpers Ferry, West Virginia, as a getaway from Old Town, in a home we owned and were setting up to list as an Airbnb rental. We went on long hikes, enjoyed the local restaurants, breweries, and wineries, and listened to music on our deck on the river until the sun went down. We enjoyed being at our Harper's Ferry house so much that we could never bring ourselves to leave Sunday evening—we got up every Monday at 3:00 AM to drive two hours back to Old Town to make it home in time for me to coach my 5:30 AM Pilates class.

We worked hard every day of the week. Living in the DMV (DC, Maryland, Virginia) area, hard work is ingrained in you. It has a different pace, the hustle is real, and I loved it.

My normal weekday schedule looked like this:

4:00 AM: first alarm, snooze

4:15 AM: second alarm, snooze but start moving some

4:30 AM: third alarm, snooze but I need to get up

4:40 AM: fourth alarm, for real—GET THE FUCK UP

4:55 AM: two shots of espresso

5:00 AM to 8:00 AM: coach classes

8:00 AM - 11:00 AM: two more shots of espresso, run Jemma, and take a class at Solidcore

11:00 AM - 4:00 PM: managerial work at Solidcore (client emails, class and instructor schedules, instructor feedback, and disciplinary issues)

4:00 PM to 8:00 PM: coach classes/more managerial work at Solidcore

8:00 PM: I am in serious need of food and a hazy IPA

10:30 PM: sleep and repeat

WORK HARD, PLAY HARD

I always say I am on the cusp of someone who lives to work. The reason I say "cusp" is because when I am not working, I am extremely spontaneous and love to have a good time.

I am motivated to work hard so I can have the freedom to play hard.

This is what led to the first breaking point of my "picture-perfect life." I was in the studio one morning, a little more exhausted than usual from a few too many hazy IPAs the night before, when one of my favorite clients asked me, "What are your goals and plans with the company?"

At this point, I had worked for them for almost three years. It was a simple question, but it stopped me dead in my tracks. Not because I was tired or because of the slight hazy hangover I was fighting, but because I didn't really have any goals with my job. I loved the community and people I was surrounded by, but I was content and did not have the desire to grow out of the role I was in.

This question flicked on a light switch in my tired, hungover brain: I was comfortable, complacent, and coasting. All things that do not sit well with a personality like mine. I thrive on goal setting and perfecting the systems to meet my aims. I live for challenges and the satisfying feeling I receive when I overcome them.

I do not want to simply ride a wave—I want to surf it and do backflips on that bitch.

At that moment, I realized I was so busy working, going through the motions, the processes, and the day-to-day grind working my ass off, *but for what?*

So, when I was asked about my future goals, I paused for a while before I responded, "You know what? I do not have any, which is something I definitely need to figure the fuck out."

My client smiled, laughed, and said, "This is why I love you."

F*CK IT, MAKE MOVES

The next day, I took off work. First day in probably a year. If the studio was on fire, my director and coaches knew I was not responding. I slept in until 8:00 AM, made my double shot of espresso, and sat down on my patio with a pen and a pad of paper. It was a perfect, sunny fall morning, with temperatures that held all day, so all you needed was a light jacket to sit outside in comfort.

Jemma chased about 100 squirrels out of the yard and took naps in the sun. I sat on the patio from 8:00 AM until 2:00 PM and did not move (except to pee, because my bladder was weak from the aggressive amount of caffeine I drank all day) attempting to write my goals down.

I kept asking myself:

- Where do I see my career in a week, a month, a year, five years?

- Where do I see my relationship in a week, a month, a year, five years?

- Where do I want to be in a week, a month, a year, five years?

I did not write anything down. I couldn't because I didn't know. At 2:05 PM I finally wrote down: "Fuck this, make moves." At that moment I did not know exactly what those moves were, but I knew I needed to do *something*.

What triggered me that day was a question about my career, but it allowed me to bring to the surface toxic experiences in my marriage I had buried for years that did not align with who I was or what I wanted. I was still unclear as to exactly *what* I wanted, but I knew I could not go down the same road with him long term. I was too emotionally removed from the relationship—it was past the point of repair. Staying with him would have been detrimental for both of us because I constantly felt responsible for his unhappiness—and he blamed me for it. I felt like it was my duty to be there to help him through it all, but he was not taking responsibility to help himself.

This made me miserable—and I was not able to be a good partner, nor did I have the desire to be, because I was lost and confused; I lost so much of myself trying to serve him.

And I knew for years how toxic it was, yet I had avoided setting boundaries to make it better. I had settled for standards below what I valued.

I had pushed it all aside and had found it easier to live a "picture-perfect" life than face these toxic situations and deal with them.

Smile for the camera! I was smiling to maintain the perfect picture, but I was dying inside.

When I realized all this, I started to question my standards, morals, and values. I had no idea what I wanted for myself. Even worse, I had no idea how to get there.

At that point, I knew I hit a dead end—no road would ever extend out in the direction I was going. I was dead inside, going through the motions of life without any defined purpose. I knew that day that if I didn't make any changes, I was continuing to dig my own grave.

RIP, Kayla. Rest in pieces.

EVERYTHING FELT HEAVIER THAN EVER

After this realization, it took me a few months to make moves.

On May 8, 2020, I was sitting at the kitchen counter in Harpers Ferry, drinking coffee, and it was an unforgettable morning.

I did not know for sure that morning I was going to leave, but I knew it was coming. I had made my decision and packed all my things—the only thing I had to do was leave. But when I woke up that morning, everything felt significantly heavier than normal—the 1,000 extra pounds I had been carrying around the past few years turned into 100,000 pounds.

By this point, I had spent months trying to work things out with my now ex-husband, but life at home was only getting worse, and horrible patterns of behavior were becoming commonplace. I was at my final breaking point. I broke down crying and called my mom.

I kept my parents as far away from my marital situation as much as possible because I knew I needed to handle and figure it out for myself. My parents also raised me this way, and I respected it.

They have always wanted what's best for me. They love me unconditionally but know it's up to me to make my own decisions. They have never wedged themselves into my marriage or tried to influence any choice I made. They always have been (and always will be) unbiased; I know I can rely on them to tell me the truth.

This morning though, I needed some love, and I knew my mom could give me that. I did not say much on the phone—I just cried—and my mom listened. Moms somehow *always* know when something is wrong, and she knew something was *very wrong*.

After a few minutes of sobbing, she finally interrupted and asked, "Kayla, what are you doing? I know you've already made up your mind. Why are you still there?"

Like the question about "my goals and plans," my mom's question was another trigger, and this one hit even harder. I immediately stopped crying because I had clarity: I didn't know. There was no reason to stay in my marriage, in Old Town, or be in our home in Harpers Ferry any longer. I was fighting my gut intuition to leave, but why? With no goals or objectives for my Pilates studio management career and a failed marriage, I had no reason to stay.

So, I took my own advice. I made moves.

DISRUPTING THE SCHEDULE

I drove away from our home in Harpers Ferry knowing I would never go back. I only cried for two minutes—I had cried so many tears over the years, I was running on empty—when suddenly, one of the most calming senses of relief came over me.

The 100,000 pounds I was lugging around was gone.

I imagined myself on a giant yacht in the Mediterranean Sea, dropping that heavy load off, never to be found or picked up again. It was something I had truly never felt before; I immediately felt at peace. I was driving away from everything I had worked for: my soon-to-be-ex-husband, Jemma, my job, and several people I loved whom I knew I would not see again. I had a car full of only personal belongings, $900, no direction *at all*, and I was navigating it in the middle of a global pandemic.

It was heartbreaking but liberating.

Everything about my journey was unknown. In the past, I never would have been able to manage it. Before this, I would have an anxiety attack if dinner plans changed from 5:30 to 6:30 PM, because "it would disrupt the schedule," and I'd have nothing to plan.

I left Harpers Ferry and drove seven hours to Knoxville to be with my family. I arrived around midnight, and I can still remember that night of sleep. It felt like I had not slept in years. I woke up the next morning and didn't even need coffee (and considering how much coffee I was drinking daily up until that point, this was monumental). I had a great morning—I did a workout in my family's garage gym and talked to my mom and dad for a while on the back porch.

My parents are both strong and taught me to trust and believe in myself as they have trusted and believed in me. I know they were heartbroken for me, but they knew I would be better for it. They were proud of me for focusing on making the best out of the situation, keeping a positive mindset, and being motivated to find happiness and peace within myself again. They would always be there to support me.

It took about a week, but I finally told my parents I would not be staying with them. I knew I had a lot of work to do, and I needed to do it on my own. I wanted their love and support, but not their help.

I had already completely disrupted my entire life...why not keep it going?

I immediately started applying for jobs, and less than a week later, I was back on the road to my hometown of St. Simons Island, Georgia. I planned to stay with one of my friends and start applying for jobs there and in Jacksonville, Florida, because I wanted to be back near the beach. I also had a lot more connections because I grew up there. It wasn't too long before I had a job doing social media for local businesses on St. Simons.

I had been smiling for the camera and my "perfect life," but it was fake and inauthentic because I was dying inside.

When I smiled for *myself* and drove away from Harpers Ferry, the new me was born. It was a true and real smile, not a fake one for appearances. My journey of growth and learning to truly love and trust myself began when I decided I wanted it to.

Turning lemons into lemonade means deciding to turn those lemons into lemonade in the first place.

When life threw me "lemons," I decided to start over, so I could start squeezing them.

LEMON DROP

Change is uncomfortable. It is supposed to be. If you do not like what you are doing, change it. You do not have to do what you think you are supposed to do. It is okay to follow your own path. Normalize starting over, moving on, and following a completely new path if you feel unfulfilled. You will always be the only pilot of your own life, and you should never fear changing direction. A better destination will never be overrated.

JOURNAL PROMPT

When have you had a "fuck this, make moves" moment? How did you respond?

_____

_____

_____

_____

_____

_____

_____

_____

_____

_____

_____

NEVER QUIT
ON YOURSELF

Your time is limited, don't waste it living someone else's life.

—STEVE JOBS

....

Once you've decided to make lemonade out of your lemons, it's important to harvest the best fruit for the job.

This starts with finding the best seeds.

....

DECEMBER 8, 2017

The old me quit on myself. The old me was not confident. The old me did not trust myself. The old me had no idea what she valued or wanted. The old me was numb, lost, and suffocating in a "picture-perfect" life, focused on everyone else's definition of success, rather than my own.

The new me holds herself to a high standard. The new me is confident in everything I do. The new me continues to understand my deep-rooted values and will never lose or compromise herself again. The new me lives every day like it is my last. I trust and respect myself enough to act and change directions without the fear of failure because I know that's the root of growth and success.

Have you ever quit on yourself? Do you feel like you're stuck in a version of yourself you would want to call "the old you?" Do you want to become the "new you?"

For the old me, getting married and then divorced did not seem like an option. My parents have been married for thirty years. They were college sweethearts and athletic all-stars—my dad was drafted and is in the Coastal Carolina Baseball Hall of Fame for his performances as a pitcher. My mom was an All-American softball pitcher.

In addition to their absurdly cute college love story, they have been the ultimate display of what real commitment and unconditional love looks like. My dad traveled for work practically all my life and provided all the financial support for my mom, sister, and me growing up. My mom raised us. They both sacrificed a lot for us—my mom sacrificed her career and my dad forfeited time spent with us. The sacrifices were commitments they made to each other, and they loved each other through them.

My parents are by no means perfect, and they never created a false sense of reality for my sister or me when it came to their relationship. Even with intense hardships (like the 2008 economic recession that impacted everyone in real estate and many others), distance (my dad was in Afghanistan for four years while I was in high school and starting college), and constant change (I moved homes quite a bit growing up), my parents were resilient and always acted with a level of respect for each other that is unmatched.

Naturally, because my parents were married, I thought marriage was the next step. I also thought I wanted to get married, because I wanted a picture-perfect wedding with all the wonderful things, I dreamt of growing up, like a handsome man, gorgeous dress, and beachfront setting.

And I got all of that. The wedding was incredible.

I got married at a small chapel on Captiva Island, Florida on December 8, 2017, with an incredible beach reception. We both are blessed with amazing (and gorgeous!) friends and family that know how to have a damn fun time.

Everything about the day was perfect, except for the most important thing... the person standing in front of me.

I was naïve, had no real idea of who I was or what I wanted, and I was at fault for making the commitment of a lifetime before taking the reins and figuring it out. This lack of reflection ultimately led to a picture-perfect life that wasn't mine and took me almost three years to realize and act on.

I can vividly remember waking up on the morning of what is supposed to be the happiest day of my life and feeling nothing. I had an incredible suite right on the beach and the weather was as perfect as it could be, but I was numb to it all.

I was not excited for the actual wedding—I was hurt by my ex's actions at his bachelor party. I was numb because I did not want to feel my feelings—I was embarrassed, ashamed, and clearly marrying someone who was also not ready for the commitment.

There was supposed to be a tropical storm that day, but luckily it pushed out. Florida weather is like a painter with a temperamental brush, dabbling in sunlight one moment and adding splashes of rain the next, but that might have been the only thing I was thrilled about. My soon-to-be-husband was already on the golf course, and my mom came to pick me up for morning coffee by 8:00 AM.

My mom is even more obsessed with coffee than I am, and coffee dates have always been special to us, so of course on my wedding day, it was a must.

We went to Starbucks right off the resort. My mom ordered her typical regular coffee with enough cream to turn the whole cup white (this always leaves me questioning whether she even tastes the coffee), while I stuck with my Venti iced Americano, black. We sat on the porch briefly to talk before our hair and makeup appointments.

I had a terrible pit in my stomach because I knew I did not want to marry my fiancé, but I did not say any of that to my mom. Instead, we talked about the wedding and a few last-minute details.

Looking back now, I find it insane that I was able to suppress so deeply what I was feeling, without any real inclination of the struggles I had, to those closest to me. I remember the narrative I constantly played in my head.

No one knew I was flying through life simply numb to it all. I not only was lying to myself, but I was lying to my family about how I felt.

(Again, moms somehow know everything. My mom later told me she could sense I was not being myself and that I seemed worried. I was more than worried—I was stressed, because I knew I shouldn't get married that day, but I had no intention of doing anything about it.)

That was what I was supposed to do, right?

This thought process was interrupted when my mom teared up and said, "I am so happy for you."

Those words hit hard because I knew I was *not* happy. I was dying inside, but I thought I could work through those feelings and figure them out later, after the wedding. I did not tell my mom how her words made me feel, but instead leaned into her happiness.

That morning, my mom and I took a selfie with our coffee. I still have the photo on my phone—my mom is the cutest and is glowing, and I have the beach bride radiance, but there is an emptiness in my eyes that I knew would not be full anytime soon.

In hindsight, I went against my gut.

My relationship with him had so many ins and outs, so many he said/she said, he did/she did, and more (that can be written in an entire novel itself) that played out over the years, both before and after the wedding. All this added fuel to the fire that ultimately sent the whole house up in flames. Things were done and said, and no amount of therapy was going to fix it.

If I had listened to my gut, I could have saved both me and my ex-husband a lot of hurt. I do not regret my decision. Even though our relationship was not healthy or strong, we experienced a lot together during those years and I am grateful for that. I learned a lot about myself during our marriage.

I DON'T QUIT

When you lose enough trust and respect in someone, there is no coming back and nothing will get better. Things will only get worse and continue on a downhill spiral.

When I knew I was completely done—physically, mentally, and emotionally, I wanted out. I do not need to go into the specific details of our relationship. We were both wrong and made mistakes.

We were always wrong for each other as lifetime partners, and I knew it before we got married.

So, what held me back from starting my saga of a story then, as a runaway bride, driving off in a convertible, catching the next flight to Europe, and saying "Screw it all?"

I am not a quitter.

Leaving my ex at the altar, or even simply ending the relationship, seemed like a complete failure. It would have been like throwing a towel in on something I had spent five years building, and that was not an option. I feared failure, and I was comfortable, before the wedding and after. I do take full responsibility for not being strong enough at the time to act when I knew I should have—ultimately compromising someone I did and still do deeply care about. We were not a match, we never were, and it came to a head on May 8, 2020.

One of the most important revelations I ever had did not come until years later, after we were already divorced. It rooted back to the gut feeling I had before the wedding, and why I felt so numb, confused, stuck, and suffocated.

I did not end the relationship when I should have, because I did not want to quit the life we had together. Consequently, I ended up quitting on myself.

And I had actually quit on myself long before my wedding day.

I gave up on my dreams in college. I wanted to go into sports broadcasting. I was working at the local TV station and broadcasting with one of my coworkers, who is now a lifelong friend and an absolute badass soccer host at CBS headquarters, and I was accepted to one of the top broadcasting internships in the country.

I can confidently say now broadcasting was not my path, and I am incredibly happy I did not pursue that career—everything happens for a reason. The moral of the story is at the time, I gave up on myself. My ex gave me an ultimatum, "Do not take the internship or we break up." I did not accept the internship and stayed with my ex. That was not the last ultimatum I received from him and succumbed to. The next led me to move to DC with him, rather than finish my final year of college in South Carolina. There was no compromise, no discussion, no sacrifice, and no support for my goals. Instead, I configured my goals based on his desires. This imbalance continued throughout our relationship.

At the end of the day, I gave up and quit on myself. I finished my last year of college online (luckily, I had made enough of an impression on my professors and the entire university for this option to be specifically created for me) and moved to DC purely for him. Not because I wanted to, but because I felt like I did not have an option. I first quit on the marriage when I quit on myself.

YOU DEFINE YOUR DREAMS

In any relationship, your partner should not be the one who defines your dreams, goals, aspirations, etc. Your partner should be your support, encouragement, and inspiration to help you achieve them. Your partner should be in your life to elevate it, not make it more challenging.

Sacrifices are challenges, but they are not ultimatums. Challenges in life will always occur, but you should always feel like your partner is on your team.

I was the one who decided not to pursue my dreams. For me to get to a point where I could deeply commit or love anyone else, I needed to learn, know, and understand how to love myself first. I needed to learn how to not quit on myself.

I had a lot of work to do. I had ignored my gut on my wedding day, but when I left my life in Harpers Ferry, I made the commitment to myself to do it. I never wanted to lose myself again in someone's vision for themselves, or what *they* thought I was supposed to do with *my* life, because I was going to be in this life for myself.

What is true about any breakup (divorce is a little messier, because the law is involved) is you learn from it and move on. You have no choice. It is a part of your past, but it does not write your future. My marriage and divorce shaped me, but they do not define me.

My marriage and divorce are only the beginning of my story. It is a catalyst, a defining moment when I trusted myself to take a leap of faith and remove myself from a situation, I knew was wrong. At first, I did not think leaving my relationship was an option, because it felt like a complete failure (purely based on societal norms). But doing so led to an enormous amount of growth, self-work, reflection, and a roller coaster ride of a journey that has brought me to a place where I feel confident, I am learning to be the best version of myself.

I still screw up daily—I am not writing this book to tell you I have it all figured out. We are on this journey of self-discovery together. I am also not writing this to say jump ship, get a divorce, and blow up everything. You are the expert of your own life. Do not quit on it for anything or anyone.

So, how did I realize I quit on myself? When did the growth, self-work, and reflection work really start?

I began journaling about three months after I left my perfect life and decided I was not going to quit on myself anymore.

Without the seeds, you cannot grow the lemons you need for your amazing, thirst-quenching lemonade.

I did not give up on myself; I searched and searched until I found my best seeds.

If you give up on yourself, you will never be able to grow.

LEMON DROP

Relationships are hard work, but they are not meant to feel like work, and they are not meant to be hard. A sacrifice as an expectation becomes an unfair ultimatum. A sacrifice as an agreement shows support. Have a strong enough relationship with yourself to know the difference.

JOURNAL PROMPT

Check-up on yourself and your close relationships. Are you being supported? Do you know what you want? Are you quitting on yourself, or have you already thrown in the towel?

_____

_____

_____

_____

_____

_____

_____

_____

_____

_____

_____

CATCH ME IF YOU CAN

He who has overcome his fears will truly be free.

—ARISTOTLE

....

You researched the best seeds for your lemonade
and searched high and low until
you found them.

But without nutrient-rich soil to plant them in,
will those seeds grow?

....

RUNNING? ME?

I grew up an athlete and have always maintained a healthy life-style. I've never put physical activity on the back burner—I've consistently worked out for over ten years now. I rarely go more than three days without exercising. Being a reformer Pilates instructor for years, this was my main style of exercise, but variety is the spice of life. CrossFit, boxing, swimming, hiking, yoga, and surfing are always mixed in too.

My physical health will always be a main priority in my life. I am addicted to the "post-workout high." For a long time, I could never jump on the train of calling it "runner's high," because I hated running—it is the one form of exercising I would not do, and it was always that way. I skipped school growing up when we had to run the mile during gym class. If I were planning a HIIT or CrossFit workout that had more than 400m running intervals at a time I made every excuse for why I did not need to do that workout and would then do something else.

The only exception I used to make was for Jemma. When I had her, I took her on quick runs, because she needed it. It was just one of those torturous things you do to yourself only for the sake of your kid (and yes, fur babies count here).

The main point is running any sort of distance was the most daunting thing I could think of.

But all that changed like a flick of a light switch.

One of my last days at our Harpers Ferry home, I needed to get out of the house. I am still unsure what possessed me to go for a run that day, but with not one cloud in the sky and over-all weather that was unmatched, I said "Screw it, sounds nice."

There was an awesome path that led to several trails through the mountains connecting to the Appalachian Trail. Flat, easy terrain only about twenty feet away from the water, and it went for miles all the way around the confluence of the Potomac and Shenandoah Rivers. The scenery was like one you would pull up on Peloton to bike through. Eight miles of an easy jog later, I had the "runners high," It was one of my favorite afternoons I have to date, and I was addicted.

During my East Coast travels of 2020, running became my sanity and a passion I was able to lose myself in. When I was running, it was as if I could go into a place where I felt like nothing in the world mattered. During that time, I did not feel any pressure, and I was able to think creatively and only for myself. I would run for only me. I was alone with my thoughts and feelings, and that gave me a sense of freedom I had never felt from any other post-workout high. Like most things that have an immense impact, there was more to it. An underlying meaning that I had not started to process—until my sister gave me the best advice I have ever received.

She said, "You need to journal."

PRECIOUS CARGO

My sister, Taylor, is one of the smartest, most intuitive, and most emotionally intelligent human beings you will ever meet. She has a double major in psychology and Spanish. She experiences life to the fullest in everything she does and has a pure soul that will light up any room. She is an energy and force to be reckoned with. She is my sister, so you can call me biased, until you meet her—you will quickly realize she truly is a rare, incredible gem on this earth.

Taylor would consistently tell me about her journaling experiences and how much processing, clarity, and rewarding feelings came from writing. And she was strategic about it. She was not forceful and didn't try to sell me on why I had to do it and how life-changing it would be. She knows I do not respond well to that, so she would subtly, for months, mention little scenarios where she found big wins from journaling.

I was not on board with this for three reasons. One, I never wrote my feelings down. I loved writing, but on factual content; not about my thoughts or myself. The idea that writing down my feelings or thoughts would help anything seemed dumb.

Two, looking back now, I subconsciously wanted to keep it all buried. I was terrified to write down on paper what I would just think through, on repeat, for miles on my run. If I wrote it all down, it would be my most precious cargo, and I would have to keep what was on those pages a secret from everyone. (Look at me now, putting it all out there for anyone to pick up and read.)

Three, wouldn't this be like a twenty-five-year-old with a first-ever, and long overdue, diary?

Yeah, I was good on that.

JUNE 12, 2020

Just like running, I finally gave in. It was June of 2020, and I was in Alys Beach, Florida, staying with my aunt to establish my Florida residency, because you cannot file for divorce if you are jet-setting up and down the East Coast. Strategically, I chose Florida because it has the shortest separation period, six months, that you could file for divorce in a no-fault situation. Plus, one of my dad's best friends was a divorce attorney there.

Staying with my aunt was the calm after the storm that was settling in following the catastrophic hurricane of my life I was trying to clean up.

She had a beautiful condo with massive views of the beach and state-of-the-art amenities—it was not a bad place to be for a few months.

One afternoon, after a full day at the beach, I wrapped up my day with a six-mile run. I was exhausted and drained from sitting in the heat all day.

Side note: it was the middle of summer in the panhandle of Florida. Why the hell was I running?

I stopped four miles in (because I was a little tired and honestly, wanted to talk) and decided to give my sister a call to catch up.

My mind had already been racing while I was running, so when she answered, I unloaded.

About thirty minutes into our phone call Taylor politely interrupted me and asked, "Kayla, will you journal tonight? Please."

I was silent for a few moments. She had been suggesting this for months, but she was pleading this time, and in a tone that made me believe I did not have an option.

It was one of those moments you remember because of a complete shift in perspective. It was like I completely forgot about all the objections and negative intonations I had behind the idea of journaling. They all went away at that moment.

I have the utmost respect and trust in my sister and the calm, caring plea in her voice made me give in. I gently said, "I will give it a try."

Her voice was calm, but you could also hear she was *rejoicing*. "Great! I cannot wait to hear how it goes for you."

I ended the conversation shortly after my agreement to put myself through what I considered hell at the time with, "Let's talk tomorrow. Love you, Sis."

JUST START JOURNALING

I made it back to my aunt's condo shortly after the conversation with my sister. I took a long shower, cooked a healthy dinner, and poured myself a glass of rosé. The aggressive heat I had endured outside all day had died off significantly, so it was a perfect evening to enjoy the condo's incredible wrap-around deck.

I sat on the couch, sipping my wine and listening to Kygo's new album *Golden Hour* for close to the 100th time. I had a note-book, which would soon become my first journal, sitting on the coffee table in front of me. I sat and stared at it, procrastinating the inevitable because I would not go against my word, while the sun set, waves rolled in and out, and people walked by for a solid two hours.

At this time, the over-thinker in me was tough to kill. I would always immediately consider the worst-case scenarios in anything. I had hesitations, driven by fear, and would go down wild rabbit holes with them. I could never see the counter or ask the question: "What good can come from this?"

My negative narrative and over-thinking, controlled by fear-driven thoughts, would practically paralyze me from "just doing" and keep me in my head.

That evening, I changed that narrative—I asked myself, *What good can come from this?* without allowing fear and negative thoughts to creep in. I knew my sister would be calling me first thing in the morning, and I felt inclined to give her a full report on my journaling experience.

So, two hours and two glasses of rosé later, I picked up that journal and just did it—I started writing...close to ten pages of complete word vomit. I am not going to put in this book exactly what was on those first pages (no one will ever know). There was no structure, there was no flow. It was raw feelings, emotions, and thoughts that had never been written down. After close to an hour of filling the pages in a notebook that would now be my most sacred treasure, the last thing I wrote was: "Stop running. Start processing."

A FEW MONUMENTAL EPIPHANIES

I came to a few monumental epiphanies within and by the end of those ten pages, with the main one being: I would never be able to outrun my feelings. I could think for miles on my run, but my mind was running without a real destination. They were just thoughts, feelings, and emotions I had without a why or a solution to process and grow from.

I recognized I was in an emotionally numb state. I had moved on, but I wasn't moving on—I had left a life I knew I would not grow in, but I was not growing. I was unavailable for myself, so there is no way I was close to being available for anyone else. It gave me clarity that somewhere along the way, I did lose myself. I did not know who I really was, and it would take a lot more work than one evening of journaling to uncover that and exactly how I managed to get to this point. I needed to "stop running" and "start processing," so I could start to uncover some answers. I needed them.

Like that night of sleep, I remember at my parents' home in Knoxville the night I left Harpers Ferry, I vividly remember the night of sleep after my first day of journaling as well.

My constantly overworked and thinking brain was able to truly rest for the first time.

I woke up early that next morning, feeling exceptionally rested, walked down to the beach, and beat my sister to the call.

It was about 7:30 AM, and she picked up on the second ring.

I immediately said, "Taylor, you are my hero. I am sorry I did not trust and listen to you earlier about journaling. I do not remember a time when I felt so good. It is hard to explain, but it's like the start of mental clarity I've never had."

She chuckled and said, "I knew once you just started you would understand. I am so proud and happy for you, Kay. Keep writing."

We talked for a little while longer. I thanked her several times for being so persistent with me, and I told her I would continue to keep her updated on my journaling adventure. After we hung up, I sat in the sand, felt the rising sun beat on my face, and smelled a light, refreshing salt-air breeze that was more rejuvenating than ever.

Like the waves crashing below my feet, an overwhelming wave of emotion crashed on me, and I broke down into tears. This was a unique emotion, and I cried differently than I ever had.

It was gratitude. I was grateful for where I was at that moment. I was grateful to my aunt for allowing me to stay with her in such a beautiful part of the US while trying to piece my life back together. I was grateful for my sister, who did not realize how much of an enormous role she played in my healing journey. I was grateful for my friends and family, who had been my strongest support system and my backbone through the low points through which I had fought. Even though I still did not know what I was doing, where I was going, or when...I was grateful.

Over the next few weeks, I continued to process the four major epiphanies (that also came from journaling) and new positive feelings I had deeper with daily journaling.

EPIPHANY #1

I lived a physically healthy life, but my mental health stayed on the back burner. I never understood how I felt or why.

I could back squat 200 pounds and run a seven-minute mile, but I was a mental wreck. I was emotionally numb. I went years without processing or wanting to process how I felt from past experiences, because burying it all was easier. But that only led me to a place where I did not know how I felt, what I wanted, or why.

I could not outrun my feelings. I had to experience and process them to not only resolve them but to grow from them. Unresolved emotions typically turn into resentment.

EPIPHANY #2

I lost myself constantly serving others. The freedom I felt while running was serving me. I needed to be more selfish before I could be selfless.

I realized this was not a reversible equation. Constantly serving others before myself had led me to fully compromise who I was. I poured myself out to everyone and everything besides myself. When I was running, it was the first time I was learning to really serve myself.

There is a reason you must put your own mask on first on an airplane if it's going down. I remember watching the videos they played back in the day of a mother putting her mask on before her child's. I remember thinking, *"Wow, shouldn't she be saving her child? He is extremely cute with a lot more life to live."* Relevant and factual, yes, but not logical. How can she save him if she is not breathing? Same concept. How was I going to be able to be generous, gracious, and helpful to others if I was not afloat myself? I needed to put my life mask on.

EPIPHANY #3

I could not physically outrun my thoughts and feelings anymore. I needed to own them, process them, and not fear writing them down. Do not overthink them, just write them down.

I realized I needed to dive headfirst into getting comfortable with being uncomfortable. Intense physical activity is uncomfortable for most people, but it has been a part of my life for so long, that it is very comfortable for me; I seek it out.

But when I first started running, it was uncomfortable. Not because of my unhealthy hate for it, but I had some grounds of comfort to work and build from. Writing my feelings down on paper was foreign. It was new, extremely uncomfortable, and I was scared.

The truth we all have heard is you have to embrace discomfort to grow and not live in fear. I did that, but it was just the start. I was severely jaded, and being alone with myself and a pen and piece of paper allowed me to uncover how hurt, lost, and confused I truly was. I am proud to say my journal experience, as simple as it seems, was a monumental breakthrough from my over-thinking with a negative narrative mentality. Not only did I just start and *keep* writing, but I also learned to apply the "just do it" mentality to every reasonable aspect of my life.

EPIPHANY #4

I was happy, grateful, and growing.

If you cut a lemon with a steak knife, you get some really rough edges. When you switch to a paring knife, the slices are smoother. Just like using a paring knife for smooth lemon edges, I was cleaning up my cut. My "rough edges" would no longer control my narrative or run a never-ending race in my mind.

I realized that no matter the circumstances, I could find happiness. I had so much to be grateful for, and I was genuinely excited for the growth I knew and could feel coming.

JOURNALING, MY THERAPY

Just like my daily run, daily journaling became what I would call "a thing," and I felt good. At first, I pulled prompts mostly related to self-reflection. This allowed me to process the self-realizations more thoughtfully I was bringing to light for the first time.

Journaling became my therapy. It is how I learned to internally process just about everything, including advice I received, moving forward. I was truly vulnerable with the pages.

Seeds need soil to grow, and to grow the best lemons, it is critical to pick a place with nutrient-rich soil—this is how the seeds will prosper.

I found my footing, my own nutrient-rich soil, through journaling. It was the only way I would be able to successfully grow.

LEMON DROP

Get comfortable being uncomfortable. Learn to express gratitude internally and externally in everything you do. Take calculated risks.

Do not hold back on yourself or overthink, just do it. You are the only one who can make the decision, physically and mentally, to grow. It is not supposed to be easy, but the reward will be worth it.

No matter where you are or what is happening, exercise gratitude and write about it.

JOURNAL PROMPT

What is your biggest fear and why? Is there something you feel you should do, but you are holding back on yourself purely because it is uncomfortable? Or are you scared?

_____

_____

_____

_____

_____

_____

_____

_____

YOUR TRAUMA IS
YOUR TRAUMA

You do not have to be fine today because fine isn't even the thing to be. Just let yourself be everything. Just be Alive.

—GLENNON DOYLE

. . . .

You have the best seeds, and you
picked the most fertile land.

What comes next?

Planting them.

. . . .

JULY 28, 2021

Hey there, just checking in with you. Now that I've given you the why for the journal prompts, I hope you have spent some time completing the first three prompts. If you are still hesitant, here is one more extremely important disclosure for you...*you do not need to consider yourself a good writer to journal. It is an exercise to get deep, intentional, and thoughtful with yourself.*

It took over a year of journaling before another life-shifting epiphany formed into words. At this point, I was establishing myself in my new career in Charlotte, North Carolina. I abruptly moved for the opportunity, received four real estate licenses in three months (which is not customary in most real estate positions), and was traveling all over to sell some of the most beautiful properties in the country.

I will dive into how this all came about later in the book, but for context, I was in a much better place—I was proving direction personally, professionally, and financially. I quickly met some incredible friends and immediately loved my job and the people I worked with. I still do. It all started with a random opportunity I took a chance on that quickly turned into my reality. I was and still am forever grateful for those who took that chance on me.

I was living in a 400-square-foot boathouse on Lake Norman. It was my godfather's twin brother's place—they both were the owners of the land development company I was working for (more on that later). They offered it to me when they offered me the job, and because I had no time to line up anything else and my start date was immediate, it made sense to stay there.

The boathouse had an incredible setup. Upstairs was a kitchenette, my bedroom, a massive walk-in shower that might have been larger than the room itself, a loft above that I turned into my closet, and a private deck. Below was a gym with a garage door that opened to its own private dock and a helicopter pad. Yes, there was a helicopter parked on it and no, this is not something I made up in my journal.

With a direct western-facing view, every evening from the deck I watched all the boats line up in front of the house to watch the sky light up every color a sunset could produce. About every evening, I sat on the deck of the boathouse, watched the sunset, and journaled.

The view from the deck is not a view you could ever get tired of—it's impossible to relay how truly brilliant the landscape was in words. The multiple pictures I took over the course of living there could not do it justice.

The journal prompt I was diving into that evening was about "applied suffering" and what that means and looks like to me. It was meant to be motivating, but I quickly realized the only suffering I felt that evening was in my mind.

Two sentences in, I wrote: "I'm currently not in the mental place. I do not have this type of hype."

I then proceed to write this:

> *Why do I feel emptiness, even when I feel so full of gratitude?*

> *Why am I so anxious and scattered when I am still able to find such "stillness"?*

> *Why do I feel nothing when I am capable of feeling so much?*

Why have I become so jaded when I want nothing but real?

Why do old scars hang around so long, they almost recreate new wounds?

Why does a little bit of loneliness take control over a lot of your life?

Why does it all subtly hurt?

Why is it just now that I am starting to recognize my trauma?

The night I wrote those words, I was drunk. I had also been crying. When I picked up my journal the next morning to read what I had written, a chill ran up my spine. It was a mess, but it was a vulnerable, *beautiful* mess. Ironically, I was not in an overall beautiful state of mind. I had called myself out for my bullshit—abusing alcohol and sex.

Before I dive deeper into this, let me go ahead and say these might be the most poetic words I will ever put on paper. What is so beautiful about poetry is within such few words, the meaning behind them is fully loaded with deep, clear content that quickly brings you to the real meaning.

I had written eight lines and eight questions of some fully loaded shit. Eight double-barreled questions that kept me in a gray area with no real fulfillment (I was succeeding and moving on, but not actually healing; I was allowing the trauma to do its thing by causing dysfunction in my life), trimming down to the final question that opened the door to start to uncover some answers.

Trauma.

We all have it, and our traumas are unique to each of us individually. No one's trauma is the same, and we cannot compare them. On a scale, of course, there are situations more severe than most of us will ever be able to understand. That is the point.

Your biggest trauma is your biggest trauma and is yours and only yours to deal with.

The only thing we all have in common when it comes down to trauma is our response. Trauma causes dysfunction in our lives when we allow it to go unresolved. We move on and bury it rather than processing and healing from it.

Sometimes we do not even recognize trauma as such until we question our behavior. We must let ourselves heal, otherwise our responses typically turn to reactions, and rather than processing, we project. Our ability to control this comes down to our level of self-awareness and honestly acknowledging how something made us feel. We take responsibility for our feelings when we can drop our ego or pride and be okay with *not* being okay long enough to put ourselves in a place to heal.

This poetic disaster I wrote that night was the trigger that made me realize my responses to my traumas were not healthy and were only going to become more detrimental. For example, I never felt good or worthy enough to be treated well in a relationship, so I attracted toxic men. When a guy came along and treated me nicely, I sabotaged it. (I go into this more a little later in the book.)

For a long time, I did not know how to be alone. When I *was* alone, I was uncomfortable, and I would fill my time drinking more than I should or with men who did not deserve my time. Rather than healing, I was hurting myself more.

CALL AND RESPONSE

Those eight questions were the catalyst for a lot of reflection.

In past moments, I had resorted to what I like to refer to as, "instant satisfaction for temporary gratification."

These reactions were distractions.

Instant satisfaction means the need or want has been fulfilled, but it is only temporarily rewarding. I also call this temporary gratification. It only satisfies the need in the moment—it provides no benefits long term and can even cause detriment if immediate desires or cheap dopamine is allowed to overpower our core values.

I have been guilty of this.

We live in what I like to call a "microwave society." We can all heat anything for a couple of seconds (or a few minutes at the most) and bam ...*bon appétit!*

It is easy these days to have what we want when we want it, just like we can reheat food and beverages in seconds.

It is easy-access everywhere, easy to take advantage of, and easy to abuse without proceeding with caution.

The countless times I questioned my decisions and actions, I journaled about it often, but never made any real change. This pattern started to wear on me. Not only did I have a ton of emotional baggage I was not working through, but I was letting it pile up with unhealthy, easy coping mechanisms. If I was stressed out, I would drink to drown it out and calm down. If I was lonely, I would call someone whom I would be better off avoiding.

Recognizing my own trauma was the key to it all; I managed to uncover some direct responses to my eight, double-barreled questions.

First and foremost, I was grateful for how I was building myself personally and professionally. For the first time I was on a career path I loved, and I had an incredible support system around me.

I was empty because of the choices I had made to try to fill voids that needed a lot more real substance than alcohol and company with toxic men would ever provide.

I was able to find "stillness" in many areas of my life. As Ryan Holiday wrote in *Stillness is Key*, "Be here. Be all of you. Be present." I was embracing who I was becoming and enjoying every minute. But with becoming all of me and being present, I was anxious and scattered, because I knew I was not making decisions I valued.

I love and care so deeply for others and want nothing but that in return. I felt empty because I would not allow myself to care how I wanted to. I was already numb, and I had been continuing to numb any feeling I had.

I wanted something real and someone who could care for my heart the way I was capable of caring for theirs, but I pushed all possibilities of that away, because I was scared to get hurt again.

Old scars opened new wounds because I gave people who did not deserve it full access to me—my body, my heart, and my soul. I downplayed who I was as a person because of it. This temporarily fixed the need and masked the pain and emptiness I felt. New scars formed with more built-up walls and continued reckless actions.

But journaling on the deck of that boathouse, I felt, for the first time in my life, I was on the right path and headed in a good direction. The sense of loneliness I felt, though, was not going away.

Knowing that subtly hurt. Not because I needed someone to fill that space, but because I could not be alone with the version of myself that relied on coping mechanisms that did not reflect my true values. They were completely hindering me.

I wanted to heal, but I knew I had a long way to go. I had only just started to recognize my trauma because up until this point, I did not really think I had any.

I quickly went from being confused and living what I would consider a whole past life to starting a brand-new career in a new city with a lot of unloaded baggage, still trying to figure out what I wanted. What I did know is I did not have it bad. Of course I didn't. I was waking up to a helicopter on the lake every morning, but mentally I was unhappy, and I was creating unhealthy habits to confront the emotional trauma that I did not even recognize was real.

This was big for me, and finally I started to clean up my act, or, in better words, get my shit together because, for the first time, I stopped comparing.

My biggest trauma was my biggest trauma and mine and only mine to deal with.

It was time for my responses to change.

HANGXIETY AND SETTING BOUNDARIES

Hangxiety and moral hangovers are very real.

The amount of anxiety or stress I had after a night of drinking and poor decision-making was never worth it. The *hangxiety*, anxiety that immediately evolves from drunk actions, and moral hangovers were crippling and stuck around much longer than any "benefit" I received from drinking when I was stressed or entertaining someone purely out of loneliness.

I cried myself to sleep often but I never let it affect work, which became my safe place. Work is where I would turn it all off; I never let my emotional and personal life affect me professionally.

As coping mechanisms, alcohol and sex had control over me. One of my favorite authors because of his delivery of powerful messages, James Clear, wrote, "You do not eliminate a bad habit, you replace it." I needed to replace mine, pronto.

I started by setting boundaries. We could argue that, for a long time, I did not know what setting boundaries meant, because I had none. It is hands down the most important thing I've learned to implement—not only in this situation, but in all areas of my life, including work and relationships (I dive even deeper into boundaries in Chapter 6). In this case, I had to start by setting them with myself.

No, I am not completely sober, and no, I am not abstinent. I enjoy a great cocktail or hazy IPA and sex, just not in the environment I was welcoming it. Now, I will not drink if I am feeling overwhelmed or stressed. I will work out, go for a walk, read, or listen to an audiobook, write, play a game—anything besides go to a bar or pour myself a drink. I love to have a great time, and I can and will be the life of any party, but I also do not need an excessive amount of alcohol to do this.

If I sat here and told you I do not go out and celebrate my accomplishments or my favorite people that would be a lie, but in my experience, extra shots that may seem fun at the time never end up being worth it. The couple of delicious beers I drink with my dad while sitting on the porch at home listening to Matchbox Twenty or a Mezcal Old Fashioned I love while at a dinner with great company has always been worth it. No matter the situation, I now prioritize the proper head space to be present and celebrate the moment before I make the conscious decision to have a drink.

I also no longer entertain someone out of loneliness. When that urge has crept in, I've forced myself to be alone and spend time doing my deepest thinking. At other times, I have or will call someone closest to me and talk through it. During these times I have done some of my best and most rewarding personal work.

What I now understand about sex is that it is meant to be experienced and explored but not exploited or abused. We should all be confident in our sexuality—we deserve to know, feel, understand, and celebrate this pleasure. But when we take advantage of the easy access, we rob ourselves of the experience sex is meant to be—an expression of deep and mutual love. When we devalue sex, we devalue those with whom we share it. When we do this, we compromise and devalue ourselves.

I find myself fortunate to understand the difference now. I know this from experiencing the extremes of the right and the wrong—and the right is *so* right. I will never again be in a situation to consider being with anyone in an intimate way for anything less, but getting there took some time. I had to dive much deeper into understanding expectations, setting boundaries, and respect, which you will read all about throughout the remaining pages of this book.

ACCEPT TRAUMA FOR WHAT IT IS

I always considered trauma as something more severe than anything I had ever had to deal with, like being denied basic necessities. I also felt that the only way to prove strength or get over something was to move on and forget about it. I denied my feelings after feeling too much.

I did not want to be hurt again, so I put up massive walls and drank and entertained out of loneliness. I went from caring too much to not letting myself care *at all* out of my own defense and protection. I experienced a lot of heartbreak in earlier relationships with men, too—they were all unhealthy because I was always the codependent partner in an enabling relationship.

Because I gave and gave and gave, I had become depleted. It had become easier to not feel and guard my heart than it was to continue to let walls down and allow for more wounds.

I was guilty of not accepting my trauma for what it was.

I lost myself completely in my marriage; my actions did not align with my values. I honestly thought everything was good, that it was not bad, when really, I was only "fine."

I have read different narratives around "fine" and now define it as a numb word. There is no actual feeling or emotional expression behind it. It is not happy or sad, peaceful or angry. If you feel fine, there is no depth to your emotions. In my experience, "I am fine" means one of two things:

You're either feeling nothing or too much to handle, so you would rather try not to feel at all.

"Fine" was the narrative in my mind because the codependent inside of me took control here. Subconsciously, I compared my problems. I was "fine," because I still compared other people's problems on a scale with mine. So, I tried to process what they were going through and how they felt, rather than addressing my own mess.

Trauma and problems do not just end. New days bring new conflicts, trials, problems, triggers, and more. We will continue to make mistakes we have to learn from.

Again, everyone's trauma is different and there is no one way to address it. What stays consistent is how you show up for yours. Not just developing unhealthy habits to deal with it and being fine, but by supporting a level of self-awareness and being present enough to respond in a way that heals.

Replace destructive habits with healthier behavior that can fulfill the same need, avoiding responses for instant satisfaction. Even though it might seem fun and reasonable for the time being, no real long-term gratification will ever come from it. Patience is an extremely underrated virtue that is usually masked in our microwave society. Since we have access to just about anything we want, when we want it, located at our fingertips (like a microwave), we are conditioned to having it all now. No quick fix can truly heal. Have enough trust and respect in yourself to set the necessary boundaries to find alignment with what you know you value and grow from there.

Without any sort of sugarcoating, this was and continues to be really hard for me. Just like all change, it is uncomfortable.

It requires a new level of discipline and commitment to a larger purpose to avoid a relapse.

I knew I wanted more for myself, in every area of my life, which would never be fulfilled by my trauma-creating actions. I wanted more than my actions for instant satisfaction only for temporary gratification would ever provide. I was ready to fully move on.

This required self-forgiveness.

I learned to forgive myself for decisions and mistakes I made that did not align with who I am. I did not hang onto them. I learned from them and let them go.

CHECK YOUR TRAUMA

When I acknowledged trauma for what it is, I stopped making false promises to myself. I set strict boundaries where I knew I needed them and committed to my present self for the future version of myself I was working toward—the one I admired for her strength to overcome these challenges. Over time, I developed consistency and commitment to doing what I told myself I would or would not do. I also stopped holding grudges and gave myself credit. I did not beat myself up, but learned and forgave myself. I also did not repeat the same unruly behavior because I messed up and felt like I could not make it better. Even though I was committed to my growth journey by focusing on making better choices to be the best version of myself, I gained confidence by reflecting on my progress and acknowledging each personal win.

Everyone's trauma is different.

Alcohol and sex were my kryptonite, but that does not mean they are yours. If you're supplementing unhealthy, hindering, or detrimental habits that are slowing your journey toward healing and accomplishing something you've always wanted, check yourself. Ask yourself the simple question, "Is it worth it?" Ultimately, you have to want to change. You are the only one who can make that decision and act accordingly. Only *you* have the power to change your actions and response.

What I can guarantee you is when you start to reckon with your deepest, darkest demons, channel growth, and start making changes, you become a force hard to reckon with. You will be more fulfilled and able to establish a new level of confidence that will help you overcome more than you would imagine.

Planting a seed is not as simple as dropping it randomly on your fertile land.

You first have to find the best place for the seed, so it gets the right amount of sunlight. When you do, *then* you can dig a small hole and plant it.

We are responsible for identifying the best place to plant our seeds—which means identifying trauma and processing it.

LEMON DROP

Do not compare your problems to anyone else's. You are responsible for your trauma only. Exercise discipline. Self-forgiveness is key. Resentment is lethal—do not hold a self-grudge for actions that don't make you proud. Learn from them and move on.

JOURNAL PROMPT

What unresolved traumas do you allow to cause dysfunction in your life? What are the steps you need to take to start resolving them?

_____

_____

_____

_____

_____

_____

_____

_____

_____

_____

_____

A COUNTERINTUITIVE PERSPECTIVE ON HEARTBREAK

I never hurt nobody but myself and that's nobody's business but my own.

—Billie Holiday

. . . .

Your seed is in the ground and in a place where it will receive the right amount of sunshine.

Now, it is time for some water.

. . . .

OCTOBER 31, 2020

Prior to my divorce, I was always in a relationship. I had a high school sweetheart (really, he was not very sweet) during my freshman and sophomore years who strung me along through my junior and senior years. I would consider this my first heartbreak experience when I learned he was dating other people. My love for him was young and immature; it came from the attachment I felt from losing my virginity to him. During my first year of college, I started dating the man who would become my ex-husband.

Even though I was always in a relationship for years, I did not know what intimacy was—I had never felt it. I was never sexually comfortable or confident. I was convinced I had some wild hormone imbalance because it was uncomfortable and I didn't enjoy it, despite my doctors telling me I was perfectly healthy. This was one of the reasons why I found the need to seek out sex when I was lonely for validation.

So, I never really enjoyed sex—until I did. Finally, there was one turning point with a man when I finally understood. *Oh...this is what it's supposed to be like. Wow, okay. Got it.*

I will call him my White Buffalo: the man who showed me how great sex could be, made me comfortable and confident (in more ways than one), and demonstrated how it should feel when a man gets off pleasing a woman. After the first time, I wanted it more and I wanted it *a lot*. I could not get enough.

In the end, the relationship with my White Buffalo was not healthy, because, the majority of the time, it was one-sided. We started out hot and heavy, but then he faded out. I wanted more, and he never said no to incredible sex, but he was never going to commit to me the way I wanted him to.

In the end, the experience gutted me. It left me completely heartbroken.

I allowed myself to care much more than I should have because of my unrealistic expectations. I was caught up in the lust for someone who did not deserve that level of access to me. When we first connected, I was in an extremely vulnerable, almost naïve, place, because an emotional connection with someone was something I had been missing and craving for a long time. I latched onto my White Buffalo because he made me feel something I never had before—intimacy during sex.

LOVE IS THE CENTER OF THE UNIVERSE

I could probably write an entire book on heartbreak alone. I have felt it in multifaceted ways, from the loss of loved ones, the ending of friendships, and the disintegration of intimate relationships with men, which is the focus of this chapter.

The famous saying, "love is the center of the universe" is no lie. When it has been stripped away from me or lost, the feelings can be just as intense. It has always been weird to me that it is called heartbreak. I am a visual person and quite literal, so when I hear the word "heartbreak," I picture a human heart shattering. (It's quite an interesting visual.) The feeling is accurate, though. It sits heavy in your chest, to the point that it can feel more detrimental to your body than a physical injury. It also lasts longer.

From experience, I know how much heartbreak can hurt. I am sure you are nodding your head "yes" right now. At one point or another, you've experienced it, like I have. The sadness, loneliness, feelings of loss, sorrow, and never-ending tears seem to have no end. So, when you can find the words to process those feelings, they can feel almost as powerful as the heartbreak itself. Even though the feelings themselves are the common denominator in heartbreak, we all cope with them differently.

In relationships specifically, I can think of one more common denominator, being a bit more of a counterintuitive perspective:

In every heartbreak, there is YOUR heart.

Read that again...and again, until you realize that no matter who else is involved, you will *always* be involved. Yes, another person is there to trigger those earth-shattering feelings, but you chose to be there. You chose that relationship, to take them back and give them more chances. You chose to stay when you knew it was harmful. You chose the one who caused the pain in the first place. You chose to fall in love with them. Ultimately, you have broken (or are breaking) your own heart and you must decide to heal.

WHAT'S YOUR HEARTBREAK TYPE?

You can never control how a person feels, treats you, or responds or reacts, but you *can* control yourself and your response to them. In every heartbreak, past or present, I am sure you can reflect and acknowledge where you were susceptible to it.

Naturally, this is not something we want to acknowledge, because of the pain we feel from it. Trust me, I get it.

Taking responsibility was easier when I started to process my complex emotions around intimate relationships and heartbreak. And then I categorized them into nine different heartbreak types:

1. The "In Love with Potential" Heartbreak: You hang on to the beginning when things were great, fixated on what could have been. You dream based on potential, and your heart breaks when the life you've planned comes crashing down. You stay in love with the idea of someone for who they were or who you believe they can be, not who they currently are.

2. The "Modern Day" Heartbreak: We want everything, and we want it now, even when it comes to finding someone. When we don't take the time to invest in a relationship, we become more accustomed to entertainment, and are left heartbroken when it doesn't work out.

3. The "Red Flag" Heartbreak: This is the heartbreak where you see all the red flags but go for it anyway. You cannot ignore the flags forever, and eventually, the toxic relationship will break your heart.

4. The "Hurt People Hurt People" Heartbreak: When someone you care for deliberately hurts you, uses you, or ghosts you, out of their own past hurt and trauma, this type of heartbreak kicks in as a projection.

5. The "Unhealthy Dependent" Heartbreak: This type of heartbreak is crippling—it controls your mind and every thought. You feel responsible for your partner's actions, and if you do something for yourself that they would not like, something bad will happen.

6. The "Cheating" Heartbreak: You find out your partner has been cheating, engaged in an affair for several years you were blinded to or comes to you after however many years to tell you they are in love with someone else. So, you go down rabbit holes of why you are not enough.

7. The "Undeserved" Heartbreak: You would give and do anything for that person, and yet you are rejected. Nothing you do will be enough. This heartbreak is the harsh, hurtful truth none of us want to accept, especially when we feel we do not deserve it.

8. The "No Closure" Heartbreak: This heartbreak comes when the relationship is over, and you don't know how to move on. You grasp tightly to the fantasy of rekindling a relationship, because there has never been a conversation that shut the door completely to that possibility.

9. The "Fear of Rejection and Failure" Heartbreak: Even though my marriage was over long before it actually ended on paper, I was scared to break up. I was heartbroken over the family and friends I loved whom I would never see again.

This list is by no means the end-all-be-all: there are many unique forms of heartbreak not included here. Heartbreak is overwhelming. This is an attempt to simplify it, so you can make better sense of your feelings.

I had two different heartbreaks with my ex-husband: The "Unhealthy Dependent" Heartbreak and the "Fear of Rejection and Failure" Heartbreak. I felt so responsible for my ex-husband's feelings, wants, and needs, I completely ignored mine. I also did not want to give up my friends or family or disappoint anyone.

I had the "In Love with Potential" Heartbreak with my high school boyfriend.

And my White Buffalo? My heart was broken in a few different ways—"Red Flag," "Underserved," and "Without Closure" Heartbreaks.

HEARTBREAK MAKES YOU STRONGER

Why can't we easily move on from heartbreak?

Because we seek a reason and answers we will never fully receive. We want understanding. To let go, we must learn to give ourselves our own understanding—our own real reason to truly let go of those people and experiences. We must give ourselves closure.

We must learn to love our scars because they taught us something and made us stronger. They will always be worth so much more than the person who left a scar in the first place. This is a beautiful thing.

Scars are permanent, and through healing I have learned to accept that some hurt does not fully go away. Rather than letting the hurt hinder me, I feel inspired. I have channeled these feelings and energy into my self-work. It has motivated me to focus and define professional success, set goals, and achieve them. Hurt has compelled me to show up better for every relationship in my life.

For these reasons, I am thankful for the hurt from *all* my heart-breaks. It has made me who I am and who I am continuing to become.

Heartbreak has taught me how to love myself more.

We all have our own experiences, stories, and traumas from heartbreak. We have scars that will always be there—some more prominent than others. Just as time causes the scars to fade, it allows the heart to heal. Once again, *you* are the one responsible for your journey. If you set yourself up to reopen old wounds, you will never allow yourself to heal and move on.

Heartbreak can make you stronger. It can make you wiser. It is an experience that can break you down to build you up. It can teach you who you are and what you want. There is so much opportunity for growth in the emotions and feelings from heart-breaks—it can bring us a new level of self-awareness and under-standing when we are hurting ourselves. It can then inspire us to take responsibility and identify what we must change for us to show ourselves enough love to *attract* the right person who will not break your heart.

If you want your seed to grow, watering it is critical. Without water, the seed will not prosper.

Healing from heartbreak is like water. Without healing, our freshly planted seed will not grow.

LEMON DROP

Your heart is in all your heartbreaks. You are meant to feel hurt to appreciate the depths of feeling love. Acknowledge the scars will always be a part of you, but you are responsible for making the conscious choice to heal, not hurt more. Hurt can inspire you; do not let it get the best of you.

There is someone who will be able to hold your heart the way you deserve, and I promise you, it is worth it.

JOURNAL PROMPT

What type of heartbreak do you have the most experience with? Are you still breaking your own heart?

_____

_____

_____

_____

_____

_____

_____

_____

_____

_____

YOU ARE NOT A TREE

Daring to set boundaries is about having the courage to love ourselves, even when we risk disappointing others.

—BRENÉ BROWN

. . . .

Fertile soil and water are essential for your lemon tree seed to grow.

But it isn't enough for it to bear fruit.
The land can't provide you with *all* the nutrients your seed needs to grow lemons.

You need to add Miracle-Gro.

. . . .

BOUNDARIES—I HAD NONE

I am an extreme person, either at zero or 100. Finding an in-between or gray area is not something with which I am familiar. This mentality has been both a blessing and a curse. When I learn, understand, and apply something, I do it at 100 percent, but it is never easy getting there. My experiences with dating and relationships have been no different.

I would not say it is uncommon to go from being married to being very single, and I did. I went from someone with a precise type and an expectation of a lifelong commitment right out of the gate to being open-minded to dating men, not a specific type, and focused on living in the moment (fun fact: I've never been on a dating app).

I had no expectations, and it was freeing, but I let myself go too far, to the point that I created another monster I had to defeat—my lack of boundaries. I stopped expecting anything from anyone I was seeing out of the fear of it being too much. I was scared it would lead to something I was not ready for. Expectations, as they usually do, always led to disappointment; but by having no standards, such as respect, boundaries became non-existent.

With no boundaries, I was not protecting myself in the present moment. And I did not even realize how weak they were. These reactions were my responses to the emotional trauma I was still holding onto. The fear of being "tied down" or stuck again. I was rebuilding, and I did not want someone to mess that up.

I had no boundaries with people I had no interest in seeing for the long term. (Let's call these relationships "situationships.")

I showed up like I would in a committed relationship, but with a lot of protective walls up. (The walls did not do much protecting.) I gave so much emotional energy but lacked any control. I was *scared* to control the narrative and set what I thought were expectations, but really were only boundaries, and hurt myself again. I was scared to have any conversation about "what we were"—I was more comfortable staying in the unknown, until I wasn't. At that point, I knew I was being used and played, yet I allowed it and played along.

The feelings I had from these types of experiences were similar to those I had when I was in Alexandria—working in circles, with no real gratification, and drowning myself in work to avoid the underlying cause of my unhappiness. I was entertaining men who were never going to be what I needed or wanted. I allowed myself to be the other girl, the arm candy, the rebound, and the booty call...*on their terms.* I became everything I did not want to be.

APRIL 8, 2023

Even with no expectations, I still felt a lot and cared recklessly without boundaries. The "no strings attached" situationships turned into loose ties that should never have been there in the first place.

One night, I hit my breaking point. I drove home from dinner at one of my favorite local restaurants, 131 Main, with one of my girlfriends. Dinner was great. We get the same thing every time—trio dip, kale salmon salad, french fries, and espresso martinis, but I had an emotional week with a situationship I was finally over. I had made excuses to drag it out long enough. I pulled into my driveway and stared at the headlights beaming into my yard. Four bunnies hopped into Gardenia Bushes, my automated flood lights turned off, and I started sobbing.

I cried, hard, for a solid thirty minutes before calling my friend and driving to her house less than a mile from mine. As soon as I walked inside her house, I continued to cry. I could not stop. After venting (and a lot more crying, God bless her), I knew changes had to be made.

My weak boundaries had created an enormous weight on my shoulders. I was trying to protect myself, but I was only *hurting* myself by accepting situations with men who were never going to hold me to the standards I held myself. I knew (and still know) how much I have to offer in any relationship, but I have always prioritized someone else's needs and desires over mine. This realization was monumental for me because this was my breaking point—I committed to not engage in situationships anymore.

I journaled about this, and one of the most incredible understandings I came to was an unspoken truth about growth: the walls that are meant to protect us end up staying up too long, and ultimately, can cause more damage. The walls I had up out of fear of commitment and being stuck and hurt again had to be let down before I could rebuild and heal by setting strong boundaries, only necessary expectations, and rebuilding respect for myself in a committed relationship.

I have always held myself to a high standard in any role I have taken on in my professional life and as a friend, sister, and daughter. Even when I was a girlfriend, fiancée, and wife it was the same.

After my divorce, why did I start to compromise these standards in my intimate relationships?

> *I lost respect for myself through my decisions and actions.*

> *I had to find a healthy balance between expectations and boundaries.*

> *I had to do some self-reflection to understand where I was going wrong.*

THE GIVING TREE

One of my favorite books my mom read to me over and over as a kid was *The Giving Tree*. (Side note: if you have not read it, *Amazon Prime* it right now. It's been voted as one of the best children's books of all time, and it truly is a classic.) The book has two characters: the boy and the tree. One of the book's moral highlights is the tree gives and gives and *gives* to the boy, without expecting anything in return, or reminding the boy of all it has sacrificed.

In the story, the boy uses and abuses this poor tree down to the final stump. He takes everything from the tree with no thought. In the final scene of the book, the boy is an old man. He hobbles over to the stump and takes a seat. The tree could be flourishing, but instead, it has been reduced to a stump. She could have gone on living if she had not let him cut her down.

This tree spent its whole life serving and pouring into the boy. No matter what it did or how much it gave, he did not care. A heavily repeated sentence throughout the story was: "And the tree was happy."

As much as I love *The Giving Tree,* I am not a tree. I will never be fulfilled by giving and giving and giving without receiving in return. I will never allow myself to get cut down without being built back up—I will not become someone's "seat" and invest emotional energy into someone who does not reciprocate my generosity.

This is not an expectation – this is a boundary for respect.

In previous intimate relationships, because I had failed to set boundaries, I allowed myself to be cut down to the stump. I am so adamant now because in all my past intimate relationships, I was always a stump. Weak boundary setting and being the "yes" girl has always been a struggle of mine when it comes to romantic partnerships. It has led to multiple situations where I've made my life harder when it could have been much easier by simply setting and holding my boundaries.

THE PROBLEM WITH EXPECTATIONS

When my ex-husband and I first started dating, I *expected* it to be long-term. And the more time we spent together, the more I *expected* him to be the one. I invested all my time and energy into the relationship from the onset because I did not think he would ever leave my life. I wouldn't have known how to move on even if I had wanted to.

I was fully invested and committed before I knew who I was committed to. I was subconsciously using what I call society's "standard timeline" as a road map.

- Graduate high school
- Go to college
- Get married
- Have kids
- Live happily ever after

This roadmap works incredibly well for many, and I am fortunate to know several people in successful relationships who followed this exact path, including my parents.

Where I went wrong was, I did not take the time to decide whether *I* genuinely wanted to follow that map. Being single and dating for an extended period was also never something I considered or thought I would do. I had never really lived alone, and the idea was uncomfortable. Because of this, I *thought* I found a lot of happiness identifying with someone as a girlfriend, a fiancée, and a wife, but that was not the case. It was another expectation I put on myself.

I never fully understood the stuck, suffocating feeling I always had that was constantly building up. I now reflect and think I subconsciously knew there was so much more for me; I was not meant to be caged within a "picture-perfect life." I later realized it was building up, because I had never tried to find happiness identifying solely as Kayla.

I focused on being the best sister, friend, coworker, wife, fiancé, daughter, manager, coach, etc. but I never went deeper than the surface to ask: What do each of these titles mean to me and why?

I was trying to find happiness in everything I *thought* I was supposed to be doing, rather than identifying what I really wanted to do for myself.

When I left West Virginia, I trashed that standard timeline roadmap, and for the first time in years, started to identify only as Kayla. I cut all strings and any expectations I had for my life went up in flames. It was extremely liberating to give myself this freedom. Simply enjoying the present moment was exhilarating, until I let it go too far in the wrong moments.

For the first time, I knew I had to find a gray area.

FINDING HAPPINESS

After self-reflecting and—I bet you could guess it—journaling, I learned a lot of my relationship experience—and lack of—were because, whether it was committed or not...

I never fully identified finding happiness as Kayla, the individual.

I invested so heavily in the person I was with because I relied on the happiness, I knew I could bring them to make me happy.

In all areas of my intimate relationships, I gave and gave and gave for the satisfaction of the *other* person.

After my breakdown with my friend, I broke it down to what I needed to work on to clear the patterns of old, intimate relationships: boundaries, expectations, and respect.

BOUNDARIES

Boundaries are processed internally and set mentally. Sometimes they do not even need to be said. They are a standard you hold yourself to—they give you the power to say no. Boundaries keep you true to your values, morals, and goals and protect you from being taken advantage of or disrespected.

This has been one of my hardest challenges. I'm extreme, remember? Going from giving everything to a clear *no* has not been a strength of mine in the past. I am learning, because without clear boundaries, we cannot manage our expectations.

I never remember *not* being a stump, cut all the way down until I had to build myself back up and grow into another tree. If I had figured out earlier how to take responsibility and set (and hold) boundaries, I would have saved a lot of time, hurt, and heartbreak.

EXPECTATIONS

I used to expect that if someone was my boyfriend, it meant we were going to be together forever. This has been an expectation because I am an extremely loyal person when I am in a committed relationship. My fear of commitment from my past relationships kept me from managing it moving forward. What

I could provide for someone else was somehow a part of me and my identity. I realized finding happiness in Kayla was missing and needed. I needed to set expectations for myself, not my "future husbands."

Dropping my expectations was freeing. I did not feel a need for a title, pressure to date, or to move fast toward any next stage in the relationship. It kept me open-minded and allowed me to enjoy the present.

It also gave me more confidence when talking to men. I did not feel like I needed to impress anyone, so the conversations had an easier flow.

RESPECT

Respect is a deep admiration for someone—for their qualities, abilities, and character traits you truly value. When I held myself to a low standard and acted against what I value, I lost respect for myself.

Like the feeling of love, you know when you deeply respect someone because the two do not exist without each other. It is reflected not only in your words but in your actions. Respect has to exist in any relationship for it to be successful, not only intimate ones.

If respect does not exist or is lost, the relationship is, too. Without respect, there is no love. Without love, there is no care. Without care, you have nothing to fight for and you move on.

Respect is the foundation of all relationships. I needed to reset and build self-respect to find happiness by investing in myself. I took a massive step back from the "dating world," because I was being reckless with my own heart—I was letting old traumas create new ones. With a lot of healing, journaling, and prioritizing saying no to people, I was able to establish boundaries and manage my expectations. I have been able to put myself and what I truly want first, before moving forward with anyone intimately. Clear boundaries are set, expectations are managed, and mutual respect is clear.

DITCH YOUR INNER PEOPLE-PLEASER

Ultimately, I was lonely and searched for that happiness in men who would never be able to give it to me.

I had weak boundaries, unrealistic expectations, and a lack of self-respect seeking happiness in someone else.

This is where I realized I fell short in the past and why, post-divorce, I continued to do so in my intimate relationships.

It also brought to light where I had unnecessary expectations, a lack of boundaries, and little self-respect in other areas of my life—I realized I still sought out pleasing others and was a "yes woman," rather than focusing on what I needed and wanted. I was checking someone else's boxes and not my own.

Does this sound familiar to you? If you are like me, you know the role of a people pleaser (in any relationship) can easily take control.

Start to ask yourself: is this checking your boxes? Are you happy with yourself and your decisions?

If not, ask yourself:

What do your expectations look like? Are they overbearing, unreasonable, or unnecessary?

What about your boundaries? Do you have any strong ones in place?

And respect? Do you have respect for the person you are with? Do you have respect for yourself?

These are not questions with quick-fix answers. They require a challenging level of self-awareness to establish and take responsibility for things we might not want to admit.

I have struggled with it all—the stories I've shared about overcoming and acknowledging traumas, hurt, heartbreak, and immense growth from experiences reflect that.

Growth and change take time. It took me years to recognize and own up to my weaknesses, and I still mess up. So, don't be hard on yourself. This process is going to be challenging work, but I promise you, it is worth it.

Just remember you are not a tree, so never become a stump. You have too many more lemons to squeeze.

Fertile soil and water are not enough for your seed. Miracle-Gro instantly gives it the nutrients it needs to grow to its full potential.

Clear boundaries, managed expectations, and respect are the ingredients that make up the Miracle-Gro you need to ensure your lemon tree is not stunted and doesn't get cut down and turned into a stump.

LEMON DROP

Giving too much of yourself will put you in a position to lose yourself. Saying "no" can be hard, but if it is protecting you, the hurt that follows saying "yes" will be harder.

JOURNAL PROMPT

Do you find yourself seeking happiness in someone else to find it within yourself? Is there an area of your life where "no" should become your default answer to protect you from this?

_____

_____

_____

_____

_____

_____

_____

_____

_____

_____

_____

_____

_____

_____

_____

7

BE CONFIDENT;
BECOME
COURAGEOUS

You don't experience life.
You only experience the life you focus on.

—TONY ROBBINS

. . . .

You added Miracle-Gro and now your
lemon tree is bearing fruit.

When it is time to pick those lemons for our tall,
thirst-quenching glass of ice-cold lemonade?

When the fruit ripens.

. . . .

THE OLD ME NARRATIVE

How are you doing? Is everything okay?

I am throwing a lot at you, so I want to check in again.

If you need a break, take it. This book and your lemonade glass in-the-making will be here when you get back.

If not:

Remember the Old Me and New Me transformations I mentioned at the beginning of the book? Let's revisit them with more context on how the transformations happened.

For years, I struggled with my body image. I was never confident in my "thickness." As I have mentioned, I have generations of athletes in my family, so my genetics are not petite. This goes back to when I was six and could not fit into anything besides husky jeans—it is when I can first remember being self-conscious about my body and I began to have a negative perspective about how I looked.

Starting with this negative self-body image at an early age meant I carried it, but it never became detrimental until years later. There was never a morning when I woke up, looked in the mirror, and did not say to myself—You're *still fat*.

Those words exactly.

This negative, Old Me narrative was at its height when I managed the Pilates studio in Alexandria full-time. I worked out daily, usually two or three times. My body was an inspiration to my clients, and I was in incredible shape. But I can assure you, *I* never saw it that way. Instead, I worked out *more* trying to lose *more* weight that I didn't have to lose.

I was focused and obsessed with a physical change when I needed an entire perspective shift. In that state, no matter how perfect I may have looked or been to someone else, I was never going to be enough for *me,* because I had severe body dysmorphia and negative self-talk that I battled in my head, daily.

DECEMBER 10, 2022

"Damn, Kayla, you look great," my date said to me as we walked to the award ceremony for my company's Christmas party. I had on a stunning white sequin gown that was perfectly tailored and hugged my body tightly from top to bottom—the back and front both had a deep V-cut, perfectly exposing the muscle definition in my back and my protruding collar bones.

We arrived at the ballroom where I would receive an award for my performance as the top sales producer for the land development company for the year (I promise I won't leave you hanging—I will build this up to much more later). At the last minute, I was preparing for a speech I was told (only a few hours earlier) that I should make. It was not mandatory, but customary, and the confidence I had from the extensive amount of hard work I put in to receive the award in the first place led me to immediately agree. Fortunately, my background in communications and broadcasting helped ease the nerves of public speaking and the lack of preparation.

The speech ended up being seamless. I received multiple compliments on my poise, delivery, and thoughtfulness. My dress was a showstopper, but the confidence that evening did not just come from the way I looked. It was the way I *felt*. I was proud of myself for a full year of hard work that paid off at the highest level. It also felt good having the courage to speak about it, and knowing I looked damn good doing it.

It was a memorable evening for multiple reasons. I had never received so many compliments on how incredible I looked, but most importantly, I believed it.

I was also twenty-five pounds heavier than the girl who could not look in the mirror without picking apart every inch of her body.

I am writing this now the same size—I am in great shape and feel amazing. My lifestyle is healthy, physically and nutritionally, and I no longer feel guilty or shut down an invite to enjoy pizza and a beer or an opportunity for dessert with friends (shout out to all of you with a hell of a sweet tooth like me). I embrace love and appreciate the healthy, strong body God blessed me with, without daily criticism.

We have all doubted ourselves, seen only the negative, and ignored the positive, whether it involves body image, looks, career, status, or anything else personally close to you. This is the negative "Old Me" narrative, and I've been in every single one of those realms. I lived in this headspace for years.

When you view yourself negatively, it becomes how you identify yourself—it becomes your reality. Whatever the real, hard facts might be, if this is your mindset, they are not relevant. This narrative can be controlled by allowing what other people think about you to be a driving factor, causing you to question your worth and what you have to offer to someone or something.

It is tough out there, I know—we are surrounded by perfectionism, especially with social media at our fingertips. We have access to it every minute of every day if we want it. It is so easy to go down a rabbit hole, and very quickly over-analyze just about everything. We set extremely lofty standards and expectations based on what we constantly see and absorb. When these standards and expectations become unrealistic because we are comparing ourselves to others, we find ourselves in a place where we feel we are constantly failing.

In reality, we are only failing *ourselves* by making this our practice.

One exercise I have found helpful to combat this narrative is to think of all the negative things you say to yourself.

Then, say them aloud.

Finally, decide whether you would tell any of them to the people you love the most.

Saying them aloud is the key. When I did this the first time, I was extremely uncomfortable with the idea of ever saying the words that came out of my mouth to my parents, sister, or closest friends. It made me a bit sick to my stomach simply imagining the scenario. I also realized my thoughts picked apart every inch of my physical appearance and how it could be improved. They consumed my every thought, so I automatically neglected who I was inside.

Anyone who knows me now might think someone else stepped in to write the first part of this section, because I am well-known as an energy with unmatched confidence and positivity among my friends, peers, coworkers, and in any social environment. I wear it. I can come on strong, and people are drawn to me for it. When I walk into a room, you know it. I am the most loving, caring, and genuine person you will meet. That is what glows.

What switched? I stopped obsessing over my physical appearance. I focused on what I had to offer as a person, what I wanted, and what I was capable of, and I made things happen. I stopped comparing myself to what I considered ideally perfect and worrying about the judgment of others. I did not want to stay in an emotionally draining head space or give up what I wanted, at the compromise of someone's opinion that was nothing but detrimental to me.

The Old Me narrative has evolved and will still try to show up, but now I quickly identify when that happens and shut it down. I remove negativity and fear. I remind myself that I am *more* than enough for me, in every realm.

THE NEW ME NARRATIVE

The confident, New Me narrative is not brand-new. It used to be the Old Me narrative. Let me explain.

I have not been in the Old Me narrative I just described my entire life—I became that during my marriage. Before that, I was confident. When I was in college, I was pursuing a career I wanted, but that changed when I stopped making decisions for myself, which put me in a negative mindset. That led to my unhealthy obsession with my body.

I was confident in my decision when I finally decided to leave West Virginia. The real New Me narrative was back. The act of leaving itself was courageous, and I did not acknowledge it at the time. I sometimes reflect on that courage now when I find myself questioning my decisions.

I received a lot of criticism and judgment for my decisions and actions to "just leave."

"Why aren't you going to therapy?"

"Why wouldn't you stay and try to make it work?"

"Why are you giving up?"

"You made a lifetime commitment. Do you not take marriage seriously?"

"Do you think you are making a mistake?"

"What about him?"

I fielded all these questions. From the outside looking in, my decision was abrupt to most, so a lot of people assumed the worst—and wrongfully so. I did not expect anyone to agree or understand—I was not searching for approval.

When I finally was able to stop obsessing about how I looked or what anyone's opinion and judgment of me was, I started making mental and emotional breakthroughs. I did not seek validation in my decisions, I made them confidently.

The confident narrative takes precedence when you value your own narrative over others enough to recognize your worth. Then you give yourself permission to follow through with what you promised yourself you would do.

None of us will be confident in everything we do, but it is up to us to make decisions in our lives to keep ourselves out of environments that foster negativity.

Confidence is powerful and positivity breeds confidence.

THINKING CONFIDENTLY, ACTING COURAGEOUSLY

The Old Me narrative is negative and fearful. The New Me narrative is positive and confident. These are the two major distinctions between the two.

Our thoughts turn to words, which become actions that create our reality. So, our thoughts control our reality. This is why the clear distinction between a positive and negative mindset is critical to identifying the life you choose to live daily.

I can identify multiple situations where I have not been confident, but when I stay in a positive, New Me mindset, I can grow real internal confidence and become courageous.

Real internal confidence starts with self-talk and becomes who you are through your words and presence—physically, socially, morally, emotionally, intellectually, and spiritually.

Real confidence is not developed by seeking outward validation. It is internally practiced by recognizing what we have in this world and ourselves, and what and who we care about most.

Real confidence is established with daily habits that build an individually fulfilling life—one that does not only bring you happiness, but pure joy and bliss that you can share with others.

Consistent, confident self-talk narratives lead to real confidence. Real confidence leads to courage. Courage leads to action.

Courage is cultivated through the actions you take, without being hindered by fear, because of the real confidence you have in yourself.

This process is not drastic. It happens with subtle shifts of thoughts, actions, and wins over time.

You will become resilient, self-aware, and unapologetically yourself. You will do the right thing and take responsibility for it, even if it is unpopular. You will exercise self-forgiveness and allow yourself to feel and process emotions without guilt or attachment. You will become open-minded and have a mentality of growth. You will live with purpose and meaning, guided by your inner truths, holding true to your values and authentic self without feeling the need to validate them. You also will not be afraid to share them, because you are unconcerned about judgment or criticism from others.

When you become courageous, you become a powerful force in this fearful world.

Developing real confidence and becoming courageous requires self-awareness—your mental narrative constructs this. Prioritizing positivity and removing negativity is the reality where we all have the opportunity to thrive.

The best lemonade needs ripe lemons. If they are not ripe when you pick them, there won't be enough juice to squeeze.

Courage is built with a foundation of real confidence. And it starts with a positive mindset. Without it, all you are doing is trying to squeeze unripe lemons.

LEMON DROP

Prioritize positivity and remove negativity. Your own mental narrative is either your strongest asset or your Achilles' heel.

JOURNAL PROMPT

Do you have a positive mindset? If not, what are three positive affirmations you can start telling yourself to become more confident?

_____

_____

_____

_____

_____

_____

_____

_____

_____

_____

_____

_____

_____

_____

8

EMBRACING
THE UNKNOWN

*Personal development—the never-ending chance to
improve not only yourself but also to attract
opportunities and affect others.*

—JIM ROHN

....

Once you've ripened your lemons,
it's time to pick them. What's tricky about this step
is that each lemon will taste a little different,
and some will be better than others.

You have to pick more than you need
to find the best one.

....

THE PULL OF AN INVISIBLE FORCE

Have you ever been in a situation where you just *know* it is right? At that moment, you cannot pinpoint exactly why, but can feel a force pulling you in that direction. You cannot ignore this gut feeling because it will linger and never go away.

Flashback: do you remember the gut feeling I had two days before my wedding that I completely ignored? I do not do that anymore. Gut feelings are not meant to be ignored—they are meant to be trusted. I take this force seriously. This is why I was able to leave West Virginia with less than $1,000 in the bank. I ignored the gut feeling before my wedding, but I was not going to do it again. So, with no road map, I made moves. My gut instinct told me those feelings wouldn't go away if I did not leave. I could feel it. It also told me to have faith that I would figure it all out.

A gut feeling is an overall intuitive sense that something is right or wrong. It is not something that is seen or based on a specific event—it is purely felt.

Trust yourself and listen to your gut instincts.

I now understand that sometimes the most beautiful things in life are unplanned and unknown.

There will always be circumstances we cannot predict and situations that might not turn out to be anything like we expected. Normalize the fact that we do not always have to have a road map to our next destination.

ROLLING WITH THE PUNCHES

Between May and September of 2020, I was "jet-setting" up and down the East Coast between Tennessee, Georgia, and Florida. While I bounced around, I did social media for local restaurants.

On October 23rd, 2020, I was let go of my job with my uncle's Amazon DSP (delivery service partner) company, helping manage daily logistics and operations for drivers in Fort Myers, Florida. The job was only meant to be temporary, but I was expecting it to last at least until the end of the year; the termination was a setback.

I also did not have a place to live. While working for my uncle, I was able to stay with him. When I was let go, I was back to couch-surfing.

I also managed to test positive for COVID.

I will never forget my drive-up Interstate 75 that day, heading back to stay with a friend on St. Simons Island (which managed to turn into a safe haven for me at the time), and calling my mom to explain my unemployment and minimal cash on hand, that I had nowhere to live, and now had the virus the entire world feared.

"*What the hell do I do now*?!" I exclaimed in an almost-poised tone when she answered. As ridiculous as it was, I managed to chuckle.

I was not completely neurotic and did not shut down, because I did not doubt myself. I trusted myself (and my gut) more than ever, so it was easy to roll with the punches. I had overcome so much uncertainty in such a brief period, I knew I would figure something out, no matter what that looked like.

I could have thrown in the towel and had a pity party, but honestly, the two thoughts never crossed my mind. I was truly enjoying everything about my East Coast tour, even with the challenges and constant uncertainty, both in my life and globally.

But listening to that gut feeling and leaving my perfect life behind, I realized I learned more about growing in those six months than I had in the previous eight years. Knowing this brought me a sense of calm and peace during a period of extreme chaos. (I also learned my mermaid soul needs to be close to the salty, ocean air.)

When I arrived back on St. Simons, I was lucky to be able to quarantine with one of my best friends at the time, who was a rock for me the entire year. The day I tested negative, I went to a coffee shop. My extroverted, outgoing personality can only stay isolated for so long before it needs a social recharge. Social distancing was in full force, but in South Georgia, restaurants and coffee shops fortunately still allowed you inside to sit down. That same day, I ran into a gentleman I know through a few family friends and business associates. He knew some of the work I had done in the past and offered me a job on the spot to develop branding and marketing strategies for his coastal transportation and tour company.

I trusted that things would work out, rather than freaking out after I had COVID, no job, and nowhere to go. This was an opportunity to succumb to the setback and be positive that I would make a *comeback*.

I took the job, and everything in my life changed—again.

Recap: In late October of 2020, I went from having no job, no place to go, and sick with COVID to being fully employed, back in an area with a strong support system, with plans to move back to my hometown, all within a week. At the time, it was the greatest thing that had happened to me in a while. Little did I know, it was only the beginning—this opportunity turned out to be a segue to the next, even bigger opportunity.

JANUARY 25, 2021

At the end of 2020, I continued my East Coast travels, because I was working remotely until I could move to the island full-time by early February of 2021. After the holidays, I needed to establish a routine throughout January to focus on my new job and to prepare myself for the move. This required me to stay in one place for more than a few days, and I was still adamant about not going home and having my own space, so I revisited a conversation my godfather and I had a few months earlier.

For Thanksgiving, my sister and I had made a trip to see my godfather and his partner at their home on Lake Norman in Cornelius, North Carolina. Both have been a huge part of my life since birth. Before this visit, the last time I saw them was at my wedding almost three years prior.

My godfather is one of the most successful and smartest businessmen I know. My godfather and his twin brother are founders of a prominent land development company and own and develop properties and communities all over the country. It is an extremely niche style of real estate, on a macro and micro level, from the land acquisition, infrastructure and amenity development, asset diversity, down to the actual sales of the property. Their visions have proved successful for over thirty years, and they continue to not only develop residential communities but invest in areas developing a luxury lifestyle. They do not only invest in plots of land for people to buy—they work to develop and invest in the areas and make them communities, adding state-of-the-art amenities, wineries, and restaurants, as well as hosting concerts and events.

Now, foreshadowing, the job *itself* is quite a lifestyle. It is a constant grind. I am always traveling, constantly adjusting to changing projects, overcoming objections, and the list goes on and on. The job is very unorthodox.

My godfather traveled back and forth weekly to one of their mountain developments in Cashiers, North Carolina. I knew they hired a sitter for their cat, Sammy, so I offered to be their designated cat sitter for January if I could stay at their home for the month. They agreed. This allowed me to focus on getting organized for my new role and finding a place to live on St. Simons Island.

It was the greatest kick-off to 2021 I could have asked for—a fresh start in a new year. I was able to establish a subtle routine over the four weeks and decompress a little. I can still remember the anxious feeling I had during this time because it was completely different from the detrimental anxious feelings I used to experience. This feeling stemmed from excitement.

The thought that surfaced in my mind daily was, *"I have a feeling this is going to be a really good year."* Maybe I was eager about the fact that, while I was there, I had established a place to live on the island, picked up a side job with the local magazine, and was scheduled to move into my new home on St. Simons on January 29th. It was the first time since I left Harpers Ferry that I felt as though I had a real plan. Or maybe, I was excited because I subconsciously felt something bigger was coming—because it was.

I was fortunate to spend a little time with my godfather while I was staying with him. He is someone I have always had the utmost love and respect for, and his credibility as a businessman is extremely inspiring, so I was eager to learn some of his secrets. We only had the opportunity for a few conversations about life, goals, and everything in between, but it was enough to have an influence.

The evening of January 25, 2021, I was making tea, and my godfather, in his calm and subtle, yet energetic tone asked, "What are you doing tomorrow?"

At this point, I was far ahead of where I needed to be with my new job and had all my ducks in a row for the move, so I had nothing to do.

I said, "Well...watching Sammy, and that is about it."

He replied, "Great. Let's go to lunch. I have something I want to run by you."

MY NEW CAREER

The next day at lunch, my godfather offered me a job to work for him and his twin brother as a property specialist and sales representative. In this role, I would be responsible for selling land in their development's all over the country.

I was immediately confused because I had no experience. But the more it sank in, the more excited I became. It also felt rewarding—my godfather saw something valuable in me. After several months of enjoying the consistent change, I was thrilled by the idea of tackling something else completely new.

I have been around the land business my entire life (a whole different story), and all I knew was I did not like it. I later realized I had this narrative because I did not understand the business yet. I also never considered myself a salesperson and did not want to be one. I was scared of the idea. Plus, I was a communications major, so I did not know anything about real estate—I had absolutely no clue how to sell expensive dirt.

I was excited to be moving back to St. Simons, too. Everything was lined up and there was certainty there. It was in a familiar area, surrounded by familiar people. It was comfortable and safe.

But even with all these well-known thoughts and feelings, something about this new—and what I truly considered absurd—opportunity, felt *right*. Even though nothing about the opportunity to take the job with my godfather's company made sense in the moment, I knew I should not walk away from it. I had committed to myself that I would not ignore my gut instincts ever again.

My godfather told me to take the week to think about it, and if I wanted to take the opportunity, he would have me meet with his brother and business partner and we would move forward from there. I took the week before I said anything, but little did he know after that thirty-minute conversation, I had already made my decision. My godfather, being the absolute expert salesman he is, convinced me to completely change paths, again.

On January 29th, I drove back to St Simons Island, but not to move there—I spent the day saying, "Thank you, but no thank you," to people and expressing my genuine gratitude for the opportunities. The next day I drove to Knoxville to pack the few final things I had at my parents' place, and my dad helped me move to the "boathouse," the first place I would call home in ten months.

On February 1st I started real estate school with the goal of receiving my license in four states before May 1st.

I had no experience in real estate, but I trusted my gut and decided to be comfortable with the uncomfortable and unknown. I was confident I would do an excellent job and saying yes to the opportunity was the right decision.

HOW I TRUST MY GUT

Another recap: I went from planning a move to St. Simons Island with two jobs lined up (one developing branding and marketing strategies for a coastal transportation and tour company and one doing social media and marketing for a local magazine), in fields that played to my well-established strengths and a strong friend group I grew up with. I turned this down and jumped at an opportunity to move to Cornelius, North Carolina, a brand-new area where I knew absolutely no one, to take a job that I knew absolutely nothing about and in an industry in which I had no direct experience.

And once again it all happened within a week.

Nothing about the decision (when written on paper) makes sense, but I trusted my godfather, the opportunity, and myself to make the absolute most of it. I trusted my gut and it was life-changing—it defined my course of success.

Trusting my gut has taught me a lot, especially how to embrace uncertainty anywhere and everywhere; and that opportunities are what you make of them.

1. EMBRACING THE UNCOMFORTABLE AND UNCERTAINTY IN ANY SITUATION OR OPPORTUNITY.

My East Coast travels helped me establish the ability to find comfort in the uncomfortable—I took calculated risks and embraced uncertainty and the unknown to the point I no longer feared it. When you know, no matter what the situation, that you can and will overcome anything, you do not fear changing directions. Writing your own road map is powerful and the amount of real confidence you establish is unmatched—this is courage and how you become a powerful force in this fearful world. This is what trusting your gut in action looks like.

This is also what holds most of us back from trusting our gut or making moves toward something we know we want. It stems from the hindering fear of uncertainty. We stay in miserable jobs, relationships, situations, etc., because they are familiar and safe, comfortable, and known.

The important thing to understand and learn to apply is that sometimes the most beautiful things in life come from embracing uncertainty because nothing about it is forced. You have no clue what is next. If you feel a pull toward making a move you are ignoring, I challenge you to throttle yourself into the discomfort of uncertainty. You will be pleasantly surprised by the comfort you will find and the new opportunities that will present themselves.

2. OPPORTUNITIES ARE WHAT YOU MAKE THEM

Opportunities are multifaceted and you can look at them one of two ways.

Without overcoming the fear of uncertainty and trusting your powerful, unignorable gut feelings, you will never put yourself in a position to receive an opportunity that truly matters to you.

If you do not trust yourself to listen to your gut instincts and have the faith in yourself to act upon them, new and good opportunities will be non-existent. Staying stagnant does not open new doors.

When you say no to your gut feelings, you will not be prepared to receive new opportunities that light you up.

When you start to trust and say yes to your gut, you will find yourself in positions to receive opportunities that align with your true self. It may not be extremely obvious at the time, but you will feel how right it is without an explanation.

Priorities change with opportunities. When you receive these opportunities, you have a choice. It is a yes or no. It is your actions and response to the opportunity that carries you from there. (This is where embracing discomfort will be critical.) This is not a one-time cycle—one opportunity will continue to lead to the next.

The most frustrating misconception about opportunities is they are assumed to only be luck. Opportunities are not just luck. You are responsible for putting yourself out there at the right time, with the right people, in the right environment.

You could be considered "lucky" to receive an opportunity but never keep to it.

If you've made it this far and you're embracing this new opportunity, now is when the actual work starts. The saying "shit or get off the pot" applies here. You cannot reward opportunities to luck when what you do with it is really the only result that matters. It can be lost even quicker than it was granted. Luck and hard work do not go together.

Your responses will put you in the position for opportunities, your actions will be what carry you through them—or not. Trust your process and never fear a new opportunity. It will always be up to you to make the most of it.

SETBACKS TO HAVE COMEBACKS

Embracing new opportunities stems not only from the uncomfortable uncertainty but also, like most things, fear. Fear of failure. Fear of judgment from others about the choices you are making that serve you. Fear is really what is crippling but when fear is present it is also important to recognize you care that much more. If you fear something, it is worth it. So, rather than being crippled by fear, how can we capitalize on it?

I call it the "3 F's": Fuck up, Fail, and Figure out. Give yourself permission to fuck up, fail, and have the opportunity to figure it out.

In other terms, you must have setbacks to have comebacks—just like you cannot understand a high without feeling low, and you cannot go up if you have never been down. It is a consistent cycle. You cannot have one without the other. This new, off-the-beaten-path road map is by no means a linear path. Paths will change, have detours, and involve a climb.

Fear has no place here.

It is much more rewarding when you can reflect on the setbacks and identify strengths that helped propel each comeback.

My setback to comeback story was just getting started.

To embrace the unknown, you have to pick more lemons than you need. I had to pick and then taste a lot of lemons to find the best-tasting ones for my lemonade recipe.

LEMON DROP

Never ignore your gut intuition. New knowledge, expansion, and experiences allow you to constantly grow and evolve. Priorities change with opportunities and comebacks follow setbacks. Fear of uncertainty and the unknown will never be a hindering factor when you trust yourself.

JOURNAL PROMPT

Has there ever been an opportunity you feel you missed out of fear of the unknown? Is there an opportunity you are avoiding now because of this? What setback might you be in that is on the verge of a comeback?

_____

_____

_____

_____

_____

_____

_____

_____

_____

_____

_____

_____

WE ALL HAVE AN EXPIRATION DATE

Don't count the days, make the days count.

—Muhammad Ali

....

You picked a lot of ripe lemons for your lemonade. You have also sliced into them to taste each one's unique flavor and selected the most delicious ones.

Now, it's time to wash and prepare the lemons for use.

....

APRIL 18, 2021

"Hey mom...whatcha doing?" I said while trying to ignore the excruciating blisters I had on my feet from the boots I was wearing, while I walked down a mountain at 1:30 AM. A phone call at this hour would not happen unless something was wrong. My mom quickly acknowledged that in her reply: "Sleeping. Kayla, what happened?"

I was at one of the land development company's mountain communities in North Carolina for the weekend learning the property. The development has around nine hundred lots, is eight miles from the front to back gate, and rises over 5,200 feet in elevation. Aside from learning how to sell lots and homes here, I also received a rude awakening—I needed to check my mountain driving skills. The roads are narrow and winding, so there is no room for error. If you screw up a little bit, you screw up *a lot*, and I did.

I was at the highest point of the development, driving across the ridge line, and coming back from a house where one of my friends was staying for the weekend with her family. I had a tour with a potential client the next morning, and I was still very new to the job and understanding the development. (When selling properties, we do not look at road names, we follow lot numbers on a plat map.) While driving, I pulled up the map on my phone I was going to need to know for my tour the next morning. I looked down for a brief second, saw a deer out of the corner of my eye, and, out of reflex, turned the steering wheel hard to the right, driving directly off the road, down the side of the mountain at a mile high.

The few moments that followed are still a blur. I had a ton of thoughts I couldn't process all at once. I went numb as I lost control of the vehicle; I was in shock. Then, my car came to a stop. About thirty feet down the side of the mountain, a boulder caught the back end of my Volkswagen Tiguan. The violent, jolted stop at about a forty-degree angle caused everything in the car to fly forward, shattering the windshield and deploying all the airbags. My driver-side door was completely smashed in by the side of a tree.

I am not exactly sure how to put into words the feelings I had in those few moments. I believe *confused* might be the only one, because the first words out of my mouth were "What the hell did I just do?" My initial thought was: *How do I get my car back on the road and drive it so that no one finds out*? (It was not that kind of mess, clearly.)

The only noticeable injuries were cuts from windshield glass on my hands and arms. With my door smashed shut, I crawled to the passenger door, pushed it open, and jumped out. The incline was so steep that climbing up using my hands was my only option.

I made it back to the road, looked down at my totaled car, and again said: "What the hell did I just do?"

It is private property, so there are no police, and we can only get help if we call for it. So, before calling my mom, I made a call to one of my coworkers, the only one I knew well enough at the time, who is also related to my godfather. I was embarrassed as I told him, as best I could, what had happened. His immediate response was also, "What the hell?" followed quickly by, "Are you okay?"

I was rattled, so he calmed me down as we talked on the phone for a little while. He told me to either call my manager or godfather to get in front of it, so I would not be in serious trouble. I called my godfather (also, before calling my mom), and his immediate concern was if I was okay. To my surprise, he was not upset at all.

I NEEDED HELP

I was still stuck on the "what the hell," so whether I was okay or not was not on my mind. I just wanted to fix it like nothing ever happened. I was disappointed in myself for carelessly looking at my phone, and the last thing I wanted was for anyone else to be disappointed in me and the outcome. But there was nothing I could do to change it.

The disappointment I felt led me to start walking down the mountain, rather than make a phone call for a ride down to where I was staying, four miles away from the bottom of the mountain. In that moment, the one thing I felt was that I did not deserve a ride. I crashed it, so walking was the only considerable option.

I was two-and-a-half miles down when I finally made the call to my mom. I came to the reality that I *did* need help getting my car off the side of the mountain. And I had a tour the next morning, so I needed a car. My mom talked to me for the rest of my walk-run to where I was staying. I made it by 2:30 AM, and my dad drove from Knoxville that night and arrived at the mountain community at 7:00 AM the next morning.

We drove back to the top of the mountain to my car. I tried to prepare my dad for the situation, but I did not do it well. I was still more worried about the embarrassment, the absurd amount of harassment I was going to receive from my new coworkers, and any other repercussions than fully understanding the severity of what happened.

At the top, my dad stepped out of his car, looked over the ledge, and stepped away. I can still remember the look on his face. Completely mixed emotions: the same "what the hell" we had all been saying, but with an extreme lightness in his teary eyes that projected nothing but gratitude.

His first words were, "You know you should probably be dead, right?"

At that moment, I did not have a response. It was something I had realized but had not acknowledged. It was a situation I understood the severity of, but I was focused on surface-level thoughts. I believe I was still in shock. Dad gave me one of the biggest hugs I've ever received, and we proceeded to take the next steps to get my totaled car off the mountain.

For a situation that could have been catastrophic if anything went slightly differently, the day went on fairly normal. We called a tow truck to wedge the car off the road, contacted my insurance company, and while all of this was happening, I used my dad's truck to run my tour.

Ironically, my clients saw my totaled car being towed down the mountain as we drove up. Their narrative was, "Wow, it looks like someone had a bad accident."

My immediate response was, "Yes, but everyone is alright." I had no intention of mentioning I was the one driving.

Since I had no car, at the end of the day, my dad drove me two-and-a-half hours back to Charlotte. The shock had not worn off yet, and my adrenaline had not stopped running. As we were getting close, he finally asked, "Kayla, are you okay?"

I said, "Yeah, I am tired and a little sore, but I am good. Why?"

Reminding me once again of the severity, he proceeded with, "You could have died last night, and you have not freaked out even a little bit. Not even once."

I paused, again. I still did not have an immediate response to his extremely accurate statement. If the boulder did not catch my car exactly when it did, thirty feet down, the decline and speed would have caused the car to flip down the side of the mountain. There would have been absolutely no chance I survived. After a few long seconds, remembering his response from the morning, I calmly replied, "I understand. I am grateful I am here."

I still did not fully understand at that moment the danger I had been in and how close I had come to a much more serious accident.

The shock eventually wore off, but I never had a full freak out or breakdown. It was not something I brushed over—I thought a lot about the severity of the situation, and how I walked away with the best-case scenario.

DEATH IS THE ONLY GUARANTEE

I had always been too scared to think about death. I was closed-minded ("It won't happen to me right now!"), which meant I never treated each present moment as the gift it was. The accident made me think deeper and in more detail about my faith.

Aside from replaying the situation in my mind a lot, I prayed, and it became clear to me that the accident was a slap on the wrist because I was ignoring other reckless actions. That realization was a punch in my face.

Something that should have been fatal left me with only a few scratches on my hands and wrists. But I could not process it, because back then, I didn't take the time to reflect and process. I was in constant fight mode, so I treated everything that was going on in my life like a speed bump I was flying over. When I thought about the importance of this experience, it was at random moments when I had small flashbacks of that night. I noticed one recurring feeling—gratitude. I was grateful to be alive and grateful I was able to think about and reflect on it.

The feeling of gratitude trickled out into multiple areas of my life—I was grateful for my family, friends, support system, job, and health, more deeply than ever before.

Death is the only guarantee in this life that unites us all. Regardless of our faith, or how different we are in our values, beliefs, or lifestyles, we all have the same fate. That means we also have the same responsibility to show up authentically and aligned with a life that works to serve the best version of ourselves.

The embarrassment, ridicule, and repercussions I was so worried about would have meant nothing if my car flipped down the mountain. I was ridiculed about the accident by my coworkers, which was embarrassing, but the jokes died off over time. That made me realize that if I had died, mourning my death would have died off, too. It puts into perspective that people forget the dead, so why live to please others?

Ultimately, facing thoughts of death forced me to think so much more about life.

When I was finally ready to reflect on and process the accident, I took to my journal and asked myself the following questions:

What greater purpose was I here to serve?

What legacy did I want to leave?

What life did I want to live authentically for me?

My "purpose" has continued to evolve, and my "legacy" is rooted in my values that I've been able to identify over the past three years through learning experiences and by living an authentic life.

These three questions are parallel and ever evolving. We are meant to feel, do, be, and see so much in this world because we are meant to be experts of our own experiences. We have the opportunity to love, see, feel, do, and be on this earth in our own unique way that no one but us will ever understand. We also have the opportunity to show up in this world and share our experiences how we choose.

It is easy to soak in all the negativity, hate, hurt, and criticism and allow it to shade how much good there is, too, and how much positive energy there is to attract. There is an incredible amount of abundance and gratitude in each of us and this flourishes when you can start identifying your purpose, acting out your legacy by living by your core values, and inspiring others to do the same.

So really think about this:

On our last day on earth, we are not going to be chasing that next dollar or title or trying to impress anyone. We are going to want to feel the earth-shattering feelings of love, joy, and kindness, and reflect on a life that we hope made a difference.

What legacy do you want to leave? You do not have to be famous or well-known to make an impact. The impact comes from where you find purpose. In a multifaceted life, it is only up to you to define and live it.

We will all die. What you believe in afterward is your faith. Have faith in something much greater and more powerful than yourself, so even when you feel like you are a complete mess, you know you are serving a bigger purpose. Death is not something that should consume your thoughts or cripple your life—it should be something that motivates and inspires you to give it all while you are here.

I was not able to process the depth of emotions associated with the accident until I started reflecting in my journal. When I did, I thought about how to experience and grow without losing sight of my purpose, which is not in a title or a final destination—it's finding the confidence, love, gratitude, and joy in daily actions.

Just like washing lemons prepares them for use, thinking about death better prepares me for life.

LEMON DROP

Forgive the past and do not fear the future. Be alive now. Be present. Be grateful and cherish each moment for the beautiful opportunity it is.

JOURNAL PROMPT

If you knew today were your last day in this life, what would make it perfect? What is holding you back from doing that now?

_____

_____

_____

_____

_____

_____

_____

_____

_____

_____

_____

_____

_____

YOU DEFINE
YOUR TITLE

Sometimes your hardest experiences can be your most potent peak experiences—which teach you lessons and provide perspectives that truly clarify what you want for yourself.

—BENJAMIN P. HARDY, *THE GAP AND THE GAIN*

....

Your lemons are squeaky clean
and ready to be sliced.

Which knife should you use?

....

DECEMBER 14TH, 2021

"I am going to be honest with you," my manager paused. He, two of my other managers, and I were in a meeting, going through my 2021 year-end review. "When you first joined our team, I never thought you would have made it to this point."

I can still vividly remember sitting in front of them and smirking, ever so slightly, to cover my real excitement. I received a lot of satisfaction hearing him passively admit I had proved him wrong. *You have not seen anything yet*, I thought.

My manager's original thoughts were accurate. As I've previously mentioned, the land business is a niche and unique style of real estate. Our entire sales team lives, breathes, and eats sales— we work nonstop. It is a heavily male-dominated industry (the few women I have been fortunate enough to work alongside are rare breeds and absolute badasses) and is extremely competitive—the definition of a shark-eat-shark environment. Dealing with a high volume of customers and clients is exhausting and emotionally draining, but if you cannot keep up, you fall off.

It has been male-dominated for thirty years now, and it is a fast-paced, and constantly changing environment. There is no such thing as being sensitive in our office. If you crumble when someone makes a joke, you are seen as weak, so thick skin is essential. Strength is proven by sales, and to do that you must manage a constant influx of clientele while learning how to master selling land. I had a lot of respect I needed to earn, and it was going to take time and hard work.

When I first started with the company, I took all of this lightly. I was fresh off my East Coast travel year, still wrapping up and filing my legal divorce documents, and learning an entire new industry, in a new place, with all new people. It was quite an adjustment I had to jump right into, and off the bat, I was unsuccessful with this transition.

Let me tell you, I made *a lot* of mistakes, and I made them quickly. Driving off the mountain was only *one* of them. (To name a couple of examples, I started an event when I shouldn't have, and I said the wrong thing to one of my managers because of a misunderstanding.) I began my new position with several setbacks, and it was on me to fix them. Luckily my lighthearted, fun spirit, ability to quickly pick up the job, and positive energy kept me in the game long enough to recover from those mistakes without getting the boot.

FOCUS ON SELLING

Shortly after my cliff jump, a.k.a. car crash, I had a heart-to-heart with the same coworker who had helped me that night.

"You need to tighten up. Focus on selling and you're all good."

At the time, I did not know what I was doing, but no one likes to help anyone new on the sales team. After I passed all my real estate courses, I still needed a lot of guidance on learning the multiple projects and developments we had—and all the traveling and adapting to new environments (my job was to sell land, remember?) was overwhelming at first, but I figured it out on my own.

It was one of those one-track mind perspective shifts. Another epiphany if you will. It made the complexity of everything so simple.

I just needed to sell dirt, and I did.

I set specific goals, developed systems to achieve them, and became laser-focused on "selling the sale," a term specific to our line of work and the volume of land we sell.

I worked my ass off and it paid off. I finished the last half of 2021 on a high note, sending me into 2022 with extremely lofty expectations—not only from leadership and my team, but from myself, too.

Being that it was my first full rookie year, I did not have a real goal or intention to win the Top Salesperson award for 2022, in the beginning. But I never doubted I was capable. Every Monday, our team receives an email with the updated "goals sheet." This displays our units and volume sold to date and is where our competitive nature is ignited. I had numbers broken down by month and year for each project. For some of the goals, I also included what I produced in the last half of the previous year.

It was around July when my intention to win changed.

I was well on track to hit my personal number's goal, and on the "goals sheet," I was also number one. I realized if I kept the same pace and stayed on track with my goal numbers, I would win.

We were only mid-way through the year with a *ton* of property to sell. We always use a common phrase— "it isn't a sprint, it's a marathon"—because you must pace yourself strategically and *accordingly*. Refuel at the correct time. Work hard, but more importantly, work *smart* to avoid burnout. If you cramp up and have to reset, you will fall way behind.

For me, that looked like: work, workout, work, sleep, and repeat. I did not take one true full day off in 2022—I was always making a follow-up call or checking emails when I was not in the office. I established a system for contacting and following up on leads that was super-efficient, organized, and that I enjoyed. I was smart about the personal tours I scheduled to meet with potential buyers and close deals. To reset and refuel after big events, I scheduled a quick trip away—usually to the beach—but I never shut down. I was always working on something.

It was full speed ahead until December. I became obsessed with winning. I identified with this. When I say obsessed, I mean losing was *not* an option. Growing up an athlete my whole life, a competitive nature is a part of who I am. When I set my mind to something, I will make it happen—if you tell me to jump, I will ask "how high?" and then jump at least an inch higher.

I set my mind to winning, and I did everything I needed to accomplish that. But I was focused on the destination, not the journey. I won, but doing so threw my life off-balance. I was left having to repair some personal relationships I neglected.

PICK OUT YOUR ROLEX

I closed out the year 2022 as the number one top salesperson for the company. I will never forget when my godfather called me into his office and said, "We've called it. With the commanding lead you have, no one is going to pass you. You are our top salesperson this year. Congrats. Pick out your Rolex."

I was relieved. I was exhausted by the end of the year trying to do everything I could to keep the lead, and this validated all of my hard work.

But what he said next was hard to hear: "It would be really impressive if you can do it two years in a row."

Rather than celebrate and acknowledge the amount of hard work and success I had that year, we were already setting expectations for 365 days later—it did not take me long to realize this would forever be the mentality with the company in my job position. It would always be "do it again."

It was a measurement of success based on someone else's definition.

We had our Christmas party at the Greenbrier, which is where they announced all the awards. I gave my impromptu speech and spent an incredible weekend celebrating our entire company's full year of hard work. It is a weekend I will never forget and always cherish because I accomplished a massive goal.

Winning also served a purpose. First, my competitive nature allowed me to thrive, but it was not what fueled me through 2022. My burning desire to win was driven by a few factors: One, to gain the respect and credibility of my coworkers by winning the Rolex. That would cancel out any doubts they had about me from the beginning.

Second, to make my godfather and dad proud. My godfather had given me an opportunity, based on his own gut intuition, to think that I could be great, and I wanted to ensure he never questioned this decision. My dad was one of the first people to work with the company thirty years ago. Over the year and a half, from mid-2021 through 2022, he became my confidant, mentor, and role model. Even when I was messing up from the start, he never once doubted me.

Third, to make myself proud. I never doubted myself, and I knew I *owed* it to myself to prove that I could do it. I could be the rookie on top, and I was. It felt damn good. Maybe years of playing competitive sports and understanding my highs and lows gave me perspective and foreshadowing on the feelings I knew were to follow.

When you are so focused on accomplishing a goal or winning, once you achieve it, you celebrate and then you are on to the next. I was so relieved when I won, I was on a high, but as soon as I was asked to "do it again" the following year, I came back down to earth. I had achieved a big goal, but it did not feel that way in the end, because I had been too focused on winning a title, rather than the journey it took to get me there.

DID I REALLY WIN?

"Top Salesperson for 2022" was only a temporary title. On January 1, 2023, we were all back to zero on the goals sheet. A full year of highly invested time, energy, and emotion was completely wiped clean. A new marathon was starting, but I was not ready for it.

I had never shut down the way I did after this year of work, and it took me a while to understand why and process that. I am not a quitter (as you know) and my competitive nature *should* have been fuel enough to defend the top-dog title, right?

Wrong. I had lost touch with my why, my purpose. I did not even know what it was. What was my purpose *now*? I had the respect, love, and support of everyone around me, and I proved to myself that I could do it. I had to re-identify what that was.

I had become so obsessed with winning, that I had neglected almost everything else. I pushed myself to the max, and I was exhausted, with no energy for anything or anyone except my job and me. I hit some big milestones within the year, including buying and remodeling my first home by myself, which I did in September to celebrate my twenty-eighth birthday, but I never took the time to acknowledge or celebrate it. I distanced myself from my family and closest friends without even realizing it. I was never present enough to enjoy the small wins. So, did I really win?

When I first took the job, as I mentioned, I never considered myself a salesperson, and I was now identifying as a "top producer." I became so obsessed with winning to the point that I lost track of my purpose because I was not present. I became obsessed more with the numbers than with fostering relationships, the part of the job I loved. That's what gave my job purpose.

A title is a surface-level identifier. Like a résumé, your job title is what is referenced, but what is meaningful is the body of work and the qualities that make you stand out. Without those qualities, your title means nothing.

We must write the body of our own résumés. We need to prioritize how we want to define our titles. That is how we find purpose.

DISCONNECT TO RECONNECT

I went from nothing to high achieving, rapidly. For the first time in my life, I was extremely stable professionally, but I felt lost. I needed to disconnect to reconnect, reset, and take a major step back. I had accomplished exactly what I wanted, yes, on the surface; but had distanced myself from what I truly valued about my position and the people around me, leaving me empty. I had a bunch of questions for myself with no real answers.

Only a few days into the 2023 new year, I was up extra early one morning. I had my cup of black coffee next to me, while I sat on my oversized sectional and dove into the book *Big Magic* by Elizabeth Gilbert, recommended by one of my coworkers, Brooke. Brooke and I think so similarly, it's strange; the countless number of times we have shown up to work wearing the same outfit is bizarre. We have the same taste in clothes and like the same types of books, so I knew it would be a great read.

It was.

Elizabeth Gilbert's passionate perspectives about creativity throughout the entire novel are amazing. One hit me like a ton of bricks as I read it:

Consider Harper Lee, for instance, who wrote nothing for decades after the phenomenal success of *To Kill a Mockingbird*. In 1962, when Lee was asked how she felt about the possibility of ever writing another book, she replied," I'm scared." She also said," When you're at the top, there's only one way to go."

It clicked. It was the fear of disappointment from everyone I had made proud. It was the fear of not being able to exceed my own goals and expectations the way I did previously. It was fear of losing everything I truly valued for another "Top Salesperson" title. I shut down because I didn't want to work toward being the top salesperson again. I had sacrificed my relationships with my friends, my family, and myself. Winning the Top Salesperson title in 2022 *served* a purpose, but winning another top title was not going to *give* me purpose.

This fear still felt paralyzing, but it was different. It was not one I wanted to take on as a challenge to overcome—it was one I wanted to break down and channel into what I felt I was suppressing.

The reason this quote resonated so heavily with me is because it spoke directly to the pressure of maintaining a top title and how it hinders creativity. It can suck the life out of inspiration and inventiveness. For me, it impacted how much I loved my job and the purpose I felt *I served*—one that cannot be identified in a title but within the qualities of my résumé that I was responsible for writing.

WHAT I TRULY VALUE

When I sell a piece of property to someone, everyone has their own unique plan—they buy as an investment, a second home, a retirement home, a rental property, or something to hold onto to gift to their children. Regardless of their plans, they have a "why."

I travel to some of the most beautiful areas of the country and constantly meet and connect with new people. I also get to be a big part of their lives, whether it is a property someone is developing for their forever home where memories will be made for years, or as an investment opportunity, I get to be a part of their why.

To break down and channel my fear, I had to bring myself back to what I truly valued: in my career it was relationships with clients, in my personal life it was relationships with my friends and family, and in my own life it was the relationship with myself. At that very moment, I was not happy with or fostering any of them. It needed to change.

Sitting there on my couch with the clarity that just struck me, I sent a group text to my mom, dad, and sister:

> I want you all to know I love you more than anything in this world. Without the small things, the big things or wins are not even worth working toward. Thank you for your love and support, always. I am sorry I have not shown up for you all recently in the same way. This changes today.

Working toward the title of Top Salesperson was not going to be my focus and goal again. I knew I would still be a top producer, but I wanted to serve a bigger purpose in 2023. By identifying and becoming obsessed with winning the Top Salesperson title, my purpose was in the destination, not the journey.

Purpose is defined in the journey, not the destination. It evolves and grows as you do. Purpose can be served but it cannot be discovered, followed, or chosen by anyone but you. You are responsible for defining purpose daily through your thoughts, words, and actions. Success is defined by purpose.

When I first started with the company, I was driven by outside validation and a temporary top performer title, rather than by what truly made me feel successful—relationships and connections.

When I understood my purpose, and that it was more than a career or a title, I prioritized myself. I also decided to be more present with my friends and family and to enjoy the process instead of chasing an expectation.

Winning helped me recognize my strengths, what I valued in my career experience, and that my accomplishments fueled my confidence to dive deeper into my passion for connecting with people.

My sales role brought me a new level of confidence. Not just because I was successful at it, but because it was something brand new that allowed me to understand and optimize my strengths. It also brought me clarity—I did not have to be an expert to try something new. I could become an expert through experience, mentor knowledge, and feedback. And trusting myself to give it a try.

The 2022 title gave me the credit I needed to excel and receive respect in the industry. It was part of the journey, but it did not define me, and it was not something I wanted to identify with. The fear I felt brought me to this realization.

Throughout my journey, some people helped, loved, and supported me. But when I focused on winning the Top Salesperson title, I neglected those close relationships, and it took a toll on me.

The question now was: what bigger purpose did I want to serve? The one I felt was hindered out of fear of disappointment, pressure, and lack of creativity?

I find purpose in effectively communicating and building relationships with new people, but also by fostering the relationships I have with the ones closest to me.

My purpose is in what I truly value about my job and was one of the main reasons I won the Top Salesperson title. I can communicate, foster, and build relationships with people. I was and have always been genuinely interested in connecting with and helping others, but not because I expected to gain anything from anyone.

I wanted to share this purpose in a bigger way in 2023, so I started writing.

When cutting lemons, it is up to you to pick the perfect knife. Finding your purpose is like selecting the right knife; there are a lot to choose from, but only one gives you a perfect slice.

LEMON DROP

Measuring success, titles, or purpose on anyone else's scale will only lead to defeat. You measure success, titles, and purpose against an internal reference point you get to define.

You choose the mountains you want to climb. Make sure they are ones you want to climb, not ones you feel like you have to. If the view at the top is the only reward you seek, you will never be satisfied.

JOURNAL PROMPT

What do success and purpose mean to you? In what areas of your life do you compare yourself to other people's scales of success or purpose the most?

_____

_____

_____

_____

_____

_____

_____

_____

_____

_____

_____

KNOW YOUR STARTING LINE-UP

And now these three remain: faith, hope, and love.
But the greatest of these is love.

—1 Corinthians 13:13

....

Your lemons are sliced and ready
to be squeezed.

Make sure you remove the seeds, though.

....

OCTOBER 17, 2023

Hi, again. How are you doing with all of this? Have you been following the journal prompts, or are you saving them all for later?

I'm checking in because I care. Some of what I'm sharing is heavy, so make sure you're doing what you need to do to take care of *yourself* during this process. This chapter is near and dear to my heart. In addition to journaling, my starting line-up is where I have been able to find comfort and support taking care of *me*.

I hope this perspective will help you understand the same.

I sat in a back left corner church pew early on a Tuesday morning. Back again in my hometown of St. Simons Island, a place that has been filled with a plethora of emotions over my lifetime, but none quite like this. It was a last-minute trip honoring the life of the son of one of our closest family friends, who passed unexpectedly.

This family is my family—I consider them second parents and their son was the closest thing I've ever had to a little brother. They own the CrossFit gym, CrossFit Grit, which has also been a second home to me for fifteen years where I watched him grow up.

We arrived at the service an hour early. I sat next to my mom and one of my dearest friends, who was also like family to them, in silence, observing every detail in the church building. From the intricate details on the ceiling to the small crack in the wood in the pew in front of me, to the slideshow of photos celebrating and honoring his life playing on two massive screens, hanging on each side of the altar.

What you could not see was the amount of true love in the church that morning and it was one of the most overwhelming feelings I have ever felt in one place. Everyone was there for the same reason: to honor his life and show their never-ending love and support for his family. The church was large, and it was fully packed with an unmatched energy and deep affection that words cannot do any justice in describing.

He was a firefighter and EMT, so the service was packed with officers who worked alongside him. The sniffles, sobs, and tears steadily continued for the seventy-five minutes we were all there diligently listening to everyone who spoke about the life he left behind. His legacy would continue to live through each soul in that building.

He was only nineteen. The saying "Only the good die young" can only go so far when a tragedy like this seems unfair. When his father spoke, he talked about one of his friends who worked as a Navy SEAL. He said to him, "I am tired of watching fathers bury their sons. Life is an unwinnable game. We must play it the best we can."

I could barely hold back tears. I felt so much hurt for his parents. I felt helpless in this situation because I knew nothing I said or did was going to make it better. His speech gave me a sense of peace. Listening to him talk about his son's life with strength and integrity gave me this sense of comfort.

Death unites us, as it is all our fate, one we cannot control.

We *do* control how we play the "unwinnable" game, and we can understand that we are not alone, because we are all playing it.

This new understanding made me feel at ease.

DEATH FORCES NEW PERSPECTIVES

In Chapter 9, we talked about how death is the only guarantee – we will all face it. When I got in my car accident, I should have died. The silver lining was that it deepened my faith and ability to think about life.

It felt like time stopped in the church that day, just like it stopped on this earth for the incredible man we were there to honor. When he died, my relationship with death further evolved. In my reflection, I found a new perspective.

We will not always get answers for why things happen the way they do. What we control in life is how we show up every day.

What kind of life do we want to create for ourselves? What kind of life should we never take for granted?

And who do we want to share that life with?

The amount of love and support that was in the church that morning was awe-inspiring. It confirmed that authentic and genuine love is the most powerful force this world has to offer. We have the conscious ability, while we are alive, to surround ourselves with people who live with this level of energy and love.

VOCABULARY OF UNCONDITIONAL LOVE

I am fortunate to have a father, mother, and sister who continue to show up daily to allow me to build my vocabulary of unconditional love. The number of long stories, examples, and simple memories of the impact they have had (and continue to have) on my life is endless. My practice of daily gratitude is deeply rooted in the love they give me, as well as the values and principles they have instilled in me through their teachings and by their actions.

My parents have displayed hard work, discipline, commitment, kindness, and resilience for my sister and me. They defined what a comeback story looks like. Because my dad was in the land development business, we had a lot, and then after the economic crash of 2008 we lost it. My dad made a noble sacrifice to support us and left for Afghanistan for the following four years.

My parents were good about staying strong and protecting us. My sister and I knew things were wrong, but we did not know the full severity of the situation at the time, because we never went completely without. I remember it was very tough, only because I saw the toll it was taking on my parents. Watching my parents suffer and lose everything they worked for, and then completely start over was heart-wrenching. The dramatic lifestyle switch was very humbling, but my parents truly never skipped a beat. Even with emotional turmoil, defeat, and failure, they kept their love and family their top priority.

Ultimately, it was a massive learning experience for our entire family. For me, it defined resilience. When I decided to start over in 2020, I was confident I could navigate, because I had seen them do it.

MY STARTING LINE-UP

My family are not the only people in my life who have shown me genuine, real love.

I also have remarkably close, life-long friends. No matter how much time goes by or how different our lives are, we always pick up where we left off, because we are committed to our friendship. If something is wrong, or we need each other, we will drop everything and be there for each other immediately.

The people we have in our lives shape us. They can make us or break us, support us, or hurt us. They create a loving, positive environment, or one that is toxic and negative.

Like sports teams, there is a specific starting lineup for every team and roster.

The people on your starting lineup are made up of those who shape you. They support you. They love you—*all* of you. Their kindness does not complete you; it elevates you. You learn more about how to love yourself because of their actions toward you. These people forgive you for things you would consider unfathomable and that you can barely forgive yourself for.

When you find yourself in a cycle of sabotage and try to push this type of support away, because you feel it is undeserved, the universe will not allow it. When someone loves you unconditionally, genuinely, and authentically, they have faith in you— they believe in you, and they do not give up on you. Sabotage is fear-driven. Faith always conquers fear.

Judgment does not exist when someone loves you unconditionally, genuinely, and authentically—only lessons of growth. They show you the parts of yourself you could not see without them: the good, the bad, the ugly, and the beautiful. Love, in its deepest form, is truly unconditional, and it is not found in the multiple. (You will not find this in everyone you meet or have a relationship with. That is why the starting line-up is small—they are your absolute best players.)

It is not simply put into words, because it lives in the actions of the people who are on your starting lineup.

My "little brother's" parents are a pure example of this. Words cannot describe the unimaginable feelings they felt for this tragic loss—words also cannot describe the impact this family has had on me. The support, love, and vulnerability they have openly shown me is unconditional; it has led me to some of the best decisions I have made to date.

They were monumental in the emotional and physical support they provided me when I left my ex. A conversation I had with them right before I left brought a lot of clarity to what I was thinking; it helped me feel more confident than ever, rather than crazy. For the entire summer of 2020, whenever I was on St. Simons Island, I also worked out at their gym as if I were a member there, like I had been over eight years ago in high school—it became one of the places where I found safety during the chaos. When I come back to visit, it is like I never left—they always say, "Your family." They truly are incredible people and the strong community they have built is still, to date, one of my favorite places to visit.

ON MY TEAM

Not everyone is a starter, but a place can be made on the roster. These are the people I value and who are a part of my inner circle. This varies from person to person, but for me, it is filled with friends, mentors, coworkers, and clients. This roster can continue to grow with opportunity, because the more genuine love you receive and have to give, the more you can attract.

YOU'RE CUT

The people who are not on your team are the ones:

- You feel the need to impress,
- Who judge you out of their own insecurities, or
- Who do not support your dreams—not out of constructive feedback, but out of jealousy.

These types of people can be obvious with negativity, or they may be attention seekers. These types of people can also be mistaken for people you would consider to be on your team or even your starting line-up. Identifying these types of people is important. Pick the wrong people and they may drain your energy and life from you.

The ones who are not obvious are the narcissists and manipulators—the ones who want to put you down to bring themselves up and who project their traumas and problems onto others because they have not resolved them for themselves. They are not capable of showing you love, because they do not love themselves. They expect something from you in return, always. It can be detrimental to other healthy relationships if you get too involved or caught up believing, loving, and trusting someone who does not have the same genuine love to offer that you do. Because the people you surround yourself with play a vital role in who you are, this can become very toxic and damaging for your relationship with yourself too. It can make you question your sense of judgment.

The amount of love I am fortunate to feel and understand through examples of role models and relationships I value most helps me recognize when it is missing. If I identify someone with negative intentions, I do not allow them to affect my presence, and I show them only kindness, in hopes they can find love in others too.

YOU'RE THE COACH

Meeting and connecting with new people come in abundance when you are genuine with your interactions. The best part is you get to choose the people you add to your starting lineup. You are the coach. You get to decide which position each person plays on your team—you also get to cut the ones who do not make it.

We are not meant to go through this world alone. Love is one of the most powerful things that controls this world. We are meant to love ourselves unconditionally. We are responsible for creating a loving environment that supports loving ourselves by surrounding ourselves with the right people—we get to choose who those people are.

We are all in this unwinnable game of life together. We choose to give ourselves daily wins and play at our full potential through everyone we have on our team. *Who do you have on yours?*

Sipping lemonade with seeds in it can ruin the entire glass, like how allowing the wrong people in your life can ruin it. Deseeding and removing the wrong people keeps your lemonade fresh and delicious.

LEMON DROP

Never take time with the people you love for granted. Never procrastinate an opportunity to share how you feel. The company you keep shapes you. Love yourself enough to know when you are in the wrong company and show enough love to keep and grow the right one.

JOURNAL PROMPT

Who are the most important people in your life? Imagine your life without them—is there something you want to tell them?

_____

_____

_____

_____

_____

_____

_____

_____

_____

_____

_____

_____

MANIFESTATION, FEAR, AND FAITH

Manifestation is not just about wishing for something;
it requires taking inspired action.

— JACK CANFIELD, *THE SUCCESS PRINCIPLES*

It's almost time to enjoy your lemonade!

To recap: you found the seeds, planted them in fertile soil, watered them, and gave them Miracle-Gro. You then let the lemons ripen before you picked them and after you selected the best lemons to use for your lemonade, you sliced the lemons, deseeded them, and squeezed.

We know we need to add ice, but that comes last. Before ice, we need to add a little sugar (or a lot, depending on your preference!).

JANUARY 18, 2023

In January of 2023, I found myself at a writer's workshop with a hybrid publishing company in Austin, Texas, taking the first step toward making my dream of authoring a book a reality. I had just won Top Sales Producer, my divorce was final, and I was still getting accustomed to my new, personal home.

I learned so much within the workshop's three days that it felt like I was there for three *minutes*. On day two, I came to some monumental epiphanies regarding the tone, voice, and structure of the book.

THE WRITING WORKSHOP: DAY 2

"I'm a mess," I typed in my notes app on my phone, sitting on an outside deck at a local bar in Austin, with a great friend from high school. We met to grab a hazy IPA—a lot about my life had changed, but my love for delicious hazy IPAs remained the same.

It was the evening after the second day of the workshop, and it had become clear that something about my book was messy right out of the gates.

When I had arrived the day earlier, I was confident in the book I wanted to write. From the moment I wrote down *Always Squeezing Lemons* that morning in the summer of 2020, I had been thinking about it, outlining some of it, and recently putting down on paper what I thought was *gold*.

But my confidence had been shattered a few hours earlier. After a few discussions with the editors, I went from loving my book to hating the entire thing—and I couldn't pinpoint exactly why.

What the hell? I thought. How could there be something wrong with the book I had worked on for almost two years?

When I left for Texas at the beginning of the week, I felt great. I was excited to finally unlock the creativity I felt I had been storing up for quite some time and take on a new challenge that felt right and authentic. As I mentioned at the end of Chapter 11, I was committed to focusing on being more present and enjoying the journey of writing the book as the purpose, not the end goal.

Despite the immensely positive energy I came with, I left the workshop that afternoon feeling extremely defeated.

I started thinking aloud, throwing around ideas for my new book structure to my friend. He sat there for about thirty minutes, diligently listening to me brainstorm as I went back and forth on multiple ideas. He gave me some feedback, but the majority of the time, he sat there as moral support, sipping his IPA with a grin—probably because he could not understand half of what I was saying, given how fast I talk sometimes, especially when I am in deep thought.

I finally stopped talking aloud and paused. I watched as cars sped by, and I paid attention to the couple in front of us who seemed to be on a first date by the way they were interacting. I turned to see the bartender pleasantly greet new customers as she poured a beer for a man who seemed to be a regular.

I remember looking down to see a weird crack in the wood of the table, as I reached to grab my glass. I then looked my friend in the eyes as I took another sip of my IPA, acknowledging how present I was in the current moment, when clarity struck.

The tone and voice of the book were all wrong because the old me was still narrating it. The new me needed to be the narrator, but I was a mess.

The old me had structured the book, too. It had been built around perfectionism and was hindering my creativity. I was smiling for the camera and suppressing the story I actually wanted to tell and the words I felt in my heart that I needed to write.

I was writing the book through the lens of the old me, and the old me lived my life for everyone else.

The new me did not make that mistake. The new me had overcome fear, failures, and heartbreak to act in strength, resilience, and confidence. The new me had replaced the idea of being perfect with vulnerability and authenticity.

BACK TO MY JOURNALS

Realizing all of this, I decided to revisit my own experiences for the content, but through the lens of the new me. I thought about this during day three of the workshop, and when I got back home, I picked up my old journals for a deep dive.

For a full day I sat and read every entry I wrote, from my first journal pages in Alys Beach to the workshop in Austin. The emotional roller coaster that covered those pages was appar-ent—an array of experiences and reflections I had captured by writing raw emotions in the present moment beautifully painted the picture of exactly how I felt, when I felt it, *why* I felt it, who I felt it with, and what it was about. The good experiences, or moments I had been looking forward to, were written in perfect handwriting. The hurt, heartbreak, struggles, and uncertainty were written exactly how I felt—a mess.

As I continued to read each entry through the lens of the new me, I could see the self-discovery unfold from the summer of 2020, less than three years prior, and it sent chills through my entire body. I was vulnerable with the pages. I did not hold back. I wrote down the truth about where I needed to heal and how I was responsible for my healing. Throughout the years, I also wrote down how I envisioned my future self.

I continue to envision my future self—the one I admire and need to become. No dream ever seems too big. I create certainty in myself, and that is powerful because I do not let uncertainty hold me back. It becomes clear how influential a committed, positive, and strong mindset is because it propels me into taking actions that support it.

This understanding all unfolded by rereading my journal entries.

Clarity was not brought to me within one specific entry—it was within the affirmations, dreams, thoughts, and beliefs I continuously wrote down.

Because what I realized is that every single one of them I had made, or was making, my reality.

I realized I had manifested everything I had been writing about for the previous two-and-a-half years.

MANIFESTATION #1: LIVE IN A LITTLE HOUSE ON THE WATER

Being close to water gives me so much life—I feel like I breathe differently in the most wholesome way. I have always wanted to live in a little house on the water—I wrote this down and thought about it *a lot.*

And I did. I moved into the boat house, and that is where I did some of my deepest self-work.

MANIFESTATION #2: FIND A PLACE YOU CALL HOME

Because I was couch-surfing for a while during and after my divorce, grounding became crucial for me. I needed privacy and my own space. The house I bought and remodeled became a sanctuary. It is a ranch-style home with three bedrooms and two baths, an incredible yard, a massive back deck with a pergola, and a concrete fire pit. It is the cutest and brings me nothing but joy to be there.

MANIFESTATION #3: FINDING A CAREER THAT INSPIRES ME AND WHERE I CAN CONTINUE TO GROW

I left my marriage with $900 in my pocket. A little over two years later, I won the Top Sales Producer award. I created great financial success for myself, but my focus was not on money; it was on inspiration and continuous growth.

My career as a property specialist allowed me to recognize my individual strengths and create an inspiring career—one that has given me endless, beautiful, and wholesome opportunities.

I view money as a tool for creating freedom, growing, developing, and helping more people. The more opportunities I have to make money, the more I can contribute to the world. The hard work I've put into earning money has been instrumental in allowing me to write this book.

MANIFESTATION #4: CONNECTING WITH PEOPLE WHO MATTER MOST

These are the people who have shaped my ideas, experience, and understanding of unconditional true love. Understanding how important the people I have in my life are. Without the love and support of those close relationships—from my parents being supportive of my divorce to my sister helping me journal, to my godfather giving me my job opportunity, and so many other examples along the way—I would not be where I am today.

This understanding is why I prioritize my close relationships and I am very particular about who I invest my energy with now, because I've reflected on the amount of hurt, I've experienced from investing in the wrong ones. The depth of this knowledge has evolved significantly over the past few years and has brought me more pure joy than anything else.

MANIFESTATION #5: WRITE A BOOK BEFORE 30

As I mentioned, I have always wanted to author a book—and now you're reading it.

It has been an emotional roller coaster but also one of the greatest experiences of my life. Getting comfortable with putting very vulnerable experiences on paper, with the only intention of helping others uncover their own hurt and trauma and grow from it is not necessarily fun or easy. Getting comfortable with the fact that every word I write is not fictional and can be picked up by anyone to read has been challenging, but I have grown more in the year writing my book than every other year of my life.

I have cried more this year than any other because uncovering my journaled feelings and thoughts required me to dig deeper and uncover and feel emotions about situations for the first time. I sat down to write this book for others—I didn't realize how much I needed to write it for myself.

MANIFESTATION #6: FIND PEACE IN BEING ME

There was a time when I did not like to be alone with myself. I lacked confidence, and fear held me back. I also struggled to forgive myself for not living up to my own standards and values, which hindered how I processed my hurt feelings. My unresolved traumas manifested as reactions that I did not value, and although I still find myself making mistakes like that, I am at peace with myself. I have learned that forgiveness, honesty, and taking responsibility are keys to finding inner peace. I can confidently say the work I've done on my personal growth has helped put me in a place where I now *love* being with me. Every day, I work to show up as the best version of myself for *me*.

A REBIRTH

When I first left my perfect life in West Virginia, I had no real direction. I was shedding layers and letting go of the old me to make way for the *new* Kayla.

I had been stagnant and mentally blocked; my transformation was a rebirth.

Nothing about it was easy. The amount of healing and growth I went through (and am continuing to go through) has been and still is extremely uncomfortable. My thoughts became my reality. It involved an incredible amount of self-reflection, hard work, focus, and sacrifice. As well as multiple unseen tears and unknown struggles. Multiple days of learning to accept mistakes, rejection, and failure as a superpower, rather than a defeat.

Through all of this, I always focused on the silver lining in each situation, or what my next step would be. It was madness to get to where I am now, but I've loved the process, I practice gratitude daily, I have never forced anything, and I have learned to truly have faith in myself and serve a higher purpose. I believe God lives within each of us and wants us to live the life we are meant to live by remembering who we truly are and acknowledging it through our actions. This does not mean perfection. It means making mistakes in order to self-reflect and grow to become the better version of ourselves we all know is there.

FEAR AND FAITH

My journal entries were my thoughts and beliefs that were reflected through my actions and became my reality. Like many others, I call it manifestation. And my faith in *me* is a big part of that.

Faith is a fundamental aspect of manifestation because without believing in ourselves, positive manifestation is impossible. If our thoughts and beliefs are negative, our actions will reflect that.

Today, I live with more faith in myself than I ever thought imaginable. When I was in West Virginia, I lived in fear.

When fear is in control, there is no faith.

What is fear?

Fear is anxiety about future situations rooted in uncertainty, judgment, failure, rejection, and change. When I finally let go of the fear of future situations I could not control, I realized I was my own worst enemy. I lived in doubt and faith in myself was non-existent. Until I had that faith, the positive results of manifestation never existed. Fear controlled my decisions.

For a long time, I was paralyzed by fear.

Fear of judgment for doing what I wanted to do versus fear of what I thought I was supposed to do.

Fear of failing, rather than taking the risk.

Fear of getting hurt and hurting others, rather than putting myself out there.

Fear of not being good enough, rather than trying.

Fear of change and it not working out the way I would have planned, rather than taking a chance and trying something new.

I constantly measured myself externally. It hurt because I was overworking myself to live up to the measure of others' standards. I was scared, and I was not living up to my own ideals.

Fear does not go away. If you do not fear something, it means you do not care enough to make a change to be less fearful. It is important to feel fear (sometimes) but critical to not let it control or paralyze you. The key ingredient to this is faith.

FAITH AND MANIFESTATION

Faith and manifestation are congruent with one another because without faith in serving something greater than yourself, manifestation is impossible.

Manifestation is a key ingredient to establishing purpose, and with purpose comes success. It compels you to show up daily through your habits, thoughts, words, and actions, as you work toward serving something bigger and greater than just yourself.

As I mentioned, I believe God resides within each of us, and we come to know Him more as we deepen our understanding of ourselves. Even if you do not believe in God, establishing a profound connection and relationship with yourself reveals your authentic self—which leads to the evolution of self-awareness and emotional intelligence.

It is our responsibility to lead a faith-driven life, not one driven by fear.

Fear dampers our creativity, limits our opportunities to believe in ourselves, and hinders our ability to create the life we deserve and are meant to live.

When I first decided to make big moves without any real direction, the only thing I had was trust and faith in myself. My faith in God evolved through this journey, but I knew I had a greater purpose to serve, and the life I was living was not authentic to who I was. For years, I realized I was manifesting a different life. I was naïve and not self-aware enough to recognize that I constantly envisioned myself doing something different than my daily reality. The major difference from then to now is that my actions did not align with my thoughts. Now, they do.

Manifestation checks in with the connection between your mind and body, and faith connects you with your true self. I express my faith by living my life within this connection. My true authentic self finds purpose through writing and sharing experiences that I have been through, knowing they can impact others.

This commitment led to the creation of the non-profit, Move Into Word, dedicated to establishing a supportive environment that advocates sustainable habits for mental and physical health, enabling young professionals to thrive. The initiative raises awareness about the power of journaling, as emphasized throughout this entire book, to empower individuals who feel lost, confused, or are searching for purpose. While journaling provides the confidence to heal, grow, and discover purpose independently, the non-profit offers a support group so individuals do not have to go through it alone.

Our self-discovery journey is not about a *new* discovery. Our mission in this life is not to learn but to *remember* who we are and live our life in *that* fullest expression—this is why I believe God is within every single one of us. This is how I continue to define success through purpose—I am, and we all are, supposed to be messengers for our original, authentic selves.

THE 3 D'S

To start taking steps toward living your most authentic life, think of the 3 D's, a concept I came up with when journaling one day:

1. Dream It: Think about the goal you want to achieve, regardless of its size or perceived realism.

2. Define It: Determine how and why you want to achieve this goal and the purpose it serves for both you and others. Ensure it aligns with your values and write it all down.

3. Do It: Outline the systems and steps you will take to accomplish your goal. Be intentional with your actions, but also be prepared for setbacks and change. Do not let challenges defeat you; have faith that everything happens for a reason. Be patient—commit to small, intentional actions that will compound over time and lead to success.

The concept is simple, but the process is the ultimate challenge. The process is what brings you to your best, highest version. Within this process, it becomes clear what you are willing to take responsibility for.

I continue to manifest daily. The faith, self-acceptance, and love I have created for myself allow me to stay committed to the vision of my best future self while disallowing past mistakes from my former self to hinder my growth. I live every day serving this and accept the completely imperfect version of myself that will forever be on a journey of expansion and growth.

How can you join this journey? By starting simply.

One of my favorite quotes is from a close mentor. He said, "Complexity is added with success." In other words, start simply, because you must just get started.

If you do not start, nothing will happen, nothing will change, and growth and opportunities will be non-existent. It is easy for us to keep our thoughts in our minds. We can all "dream it," but *defining* it and *doing* it requires taking the first step. It does not have to be and will *not* be perfect.

The idea of achieving perfection is one of the reasons why it is hard for a lot of people to start. Most people get stuck in the self-sabotage phase, which includes doubt and imposter syndrome, which are all created out of fear. Learning to accept and find joy in the journey, not the outcome, is the reward, which helps to make the idea of getting started less intimidating.

YOU ARE ALL OF YOU

With only $900 and boundless uncertainty two-and-a-half years before, I stayed positive, had faith in myself, and trusted there was *more* for me. Not "more" defined by someone else, but by me—and only me.

I created certainty and faith in myself to overcome uncertainty and fear.

When you realize what you have faith in, you recognize what you're willing to take responsibility for. You will also start to understand your purpose is not meant to be defined by one singular plan. Success is not defined by one title, and neither purpose nor success can be truly defined by anyone but you.

There is a lot of talk about having to "discover" this or "find ourselves" to understand such concepts.

You are already discovered—you are here, and you are in control. This means you get to create yourself. You already have the tools. You are the paper and pen; you get to write your pages. You cannot erase regrets, but you can scratch through them and keep writing. You get to write each present moment exactly how you would like. My thoughts, beliefs, and actions transformed into my future reality—and you have the power to do the same.

To manifest the you that you desire, understand this is internally processed and externally rewarded. If you want more, talk to yourself as if you are deserving of more. Take subliminal messages seriously. With thoughts, words, and actions, work to make what may seem unreasonable your reality. Putting yourself in the right place with the right people (people matter because your environment and proximity matter) at the right time can be life-changing when you are living your life authentically.

In Neale Donald's Walsh *Conversations with God,* he writes, "If there was such a thing as a sin, this would be it: to allow yourself to become what you are because of the experience of others." It validates that living a life that is authentic to you is your main responsibility.

If we live a life that only serves others or is defined by something or someone else, we are not living at all.

The faith you have in a higher power is your choice, just like everything else in our lives, but this message is universal—you cannot define yourself or create your most authentic life through anyone else.

Your systems, goals, dreams, and vision of the best version of your highest self, never have to make sense to anyone else. When you get to the point where you have faith in yourself and acknowledge you are deserving of more, it will not make sense to the majority of people. That's okay. You will have authentic clarity and forget this as a concern, because fear will no longer control you.

This is the final step to living an authentic life.

The final step needed to finish making lemonade? Sugar!

You get to add as much or as little as you want (I don't love mine too sweet) and that's the beauty of it—you get to choose.

Then you will be free to be who you truly are—an extraordinary tall glass of thirst-quenching lemonade.

LEMON DROP

Becoming the future version of ourselves we want to be requires us to identify who that person is, specifically, and then show up in every present moment, motivated and inspired by the opportunity to truly admire ourselves. Self-doubt becomes self-belief when we become our own greatest fans through our words, actions, and faith in ourselves.

JOURNAL PROMPT

What does manifestation mean to you? Where are you missing faith in things you are doubting?

_____

_____

_____

_____

_____

_____

_____

_____

_____

_____

_____

_____

CONCLUSION

How does that tall, delicious, thirst-quenching glass of lemonade taste?

Pretty damn good, right?

When I started to transition from the old me to the new me at the beginning of the book, I set the precedent for a journey of self-love, growth, and new understandings —a journey filled with hurt, heartbreak, mistakes, failures, and rejections, along with victories, exciting new experiences, and unconditional love and support.

I transitioned from focusing on a "perfect life," determined by external validation, to setting an internal reference point (of understanding what brings me purpose and peace and living confidently, so I can continue to grow into the most authentic version of myself) that allowed me to confidently make decisions without fear controlling my narrative. I gained confidence in myself by recognizing my strengths through my actions and accepting every setback as an opportunity for a comeback. If I screw up, I do not dwell, and I recognize that we are all imperfect humans in an imperfect world. I treat each instance as another opportunity for learning and growth. I also now understand that self-forgiveness is one of the greatest gifts we can give. I completely shifted my narrative from self-doubt to self-*belief* by replacing fears that crippled me with faith and courage that now continue to carry me in daily life.

Reflection is powerful. As I reflect on the conception of this book and my purpose, I truly felt called to share my story. While growing up, I knew I loved writing and that I wanted to write a novel, but I did not know what it would be until I realized my experiences could be a valuable roadmap for others going through something similar. I never would want someone to succumb to a "picture-perfect" life or stay stuck in a version of themselves because of the same fear I felt.

Throughout my journey, I have struggled with the imposter syndrome: *Why me? What do I have to say that could help someone else?*

If I had let that fear control me, you would not have read this book. Instead, I focused on the fact that we are all experts in our own experiences, and we all have daily opportunities to share our knowledge with and learn from others.

When I first started this book, what I did not realize was how much I was writing it for myself. When I tell people how powerful journaling is, I always say, "Be truly vulnerable with the pages," and this entire book required that of me. Uncovering thoughts and feelings from unprocessed emotions and experiences was extraordinarily uncomfortable. It was a different form of therapy, healing, and growing through revisiting and deep diving into reflection throughout the transition to the "new me."

The valuable roadmap of learning experiences I write out for you, I also continue to reference and grow from. I use my writing as strong reminders daily. I reread newsletters, quotes, and journal entries when I want to reflect or need extra inspiration to feel empowered. I write down how I am feeling and when I am feeling it so I can heal, grow, and evolve.

Personal development is not tasks on a to-do list that you can cross off and move on from, thinking they are complete or mastered. They are developed and built upon *experience*. On my toughest days, I use my experiences as resources to give myself credit for how far I've come, rather than how far away I am from the next destination. I exercise gratitude for the present moment.

I am still growing and evolving daily in everything I do, but I live every day knowing I am responsible for everything in my life. My actions, reactions, and responses are all my responsibilities, as yours are yours, too.

CHANGING MY LIFE FOR THE BEST

Why did *Always Squeezing Lemons* stick?

Because even when life felt like it was overflowing my cup and giving me too much to manage, I kept drinking and making more lemonade. I kept going, and I will never stop.

If you are living life the way you should, life will never stop throwing more lemons in your face.

My twenties have been far from what I originally envisioned, but sitting here writing this now, I cannot imagine anything being different. I have no regrets, and I can promise you that what may look like the greatest failures on paper are, from the outside looking in, some of my greatest successes, defined within.

You cannot have comebacks without setbacks, and you cannot grow without failing.

I've found comfort in being uncomfortable because I created certainty from confidence in myself in uncertain situations. There is always a silver lining; you have to be willing to look for and acknowledge it.

Be present and enjoy the journey, living as the most authentic you, because every second is worth cherishing, since the next one is never guaranteed.

Form relationships with the right people and always foster them with the people on your team. If it were not for my family and support system, I do not know if I would have found the faith in myself to take the leaps and risks I did.

Practice gratitude daily; you will train yourself to find positivity in everything.

Time is a crazy thing—this book journey started in May 2020. When I look back and think about how much has happened and how much I've grown since then, it seems like a whole lifetime ago. But the memory is so vividly clear, I remember it as if it were yesterday.

I have come to understand how quickly things change and have learned not to get caught up in the time ahead or past mistakes, but rather to focus on cherishing the present moment for the blessing it is.

Everything happens for a reason. There are many things we cannot control in this life, but we always have control over our thoughts, words, and actions—how we choose to respond versus react, or process versus project. We take full responsibility when we realize we can be the cause, problem, and solution for everything in our lives. When we can take full responsibility, our lives change for the better.

SUCCESS REDEFINED

Success is defined through purpose, something that can only be crafted by you through your habits, thoughts, words, and actions.

Without purpose, confidence remains elusive, and we succumb to a negative narrative. The motivation to grow diminishes, as staying stagnant and avoiding change seems easier. The inclination to heal is suppressed, too, contributing additional dysfunction to our lives.

We also feel stuck and suffocated without purpose, lacking a reason to fight for what matters. And without purpose, we relinquish the responsibility to define success for ourselves—we allow others to dictate our path as we succumb to fear rather than acting in faith.

You are responsible for defining what brings you purpose. Failing to define purpose for yourself leads to a life spent chasing success based on someone else's definition rather than your own.

Purpose evolves with personal growth but resides in your core values and what brings joy to your journey. Success lies in celebrating the multitude of destinations and acknowledging both small and big wins achieved by living out *your* purpose. When you live with purpose, you always win.

Now that you are done reading, identify what brings you purpose. What fills your cup with the best sip of lemonade you cannot wait to take every single day?

Be intentional with asking questions that either hinder or support your authentic life:

Are you living a life defined as successful to you, or is it based on success for others?

Can you find peace within yourself, or are you itching to go in a different direction?

Do you feel confident and supported, or negative and defeated?

Do you live in fear, or are you ready to take a leap of faith?

I encourage you to journal. You do not have to use any of the prompts I've added; just start writing. Find peace in being with yourself but know you do not have to take on any journey alone. I also encourage you to buy this book for someone else you know who wants to take steps toward personal growth and becoming the most confident, authentic version of themselves.

We all have the power to impact this world beautifully when we show up for ourselves in our truest forms. We can love, support, and inspire others to do the same.

Be you, be all of you. Be the version of you the world deserves to experience—the real you.

The old me defined success based on external measures. The new me now knows that my success can never be defined by anything—or anyone—but me.

Success is not found in validation; it is found in reflection. You do not find success in the abundance of people; you find it in the few who love you unconditionally. Success is not defined by one title—it is an ever-evolving title.

Like me, you can learn to find your strengths and you learn how to capitalize on them. You grow to understand the importance of loving, serving, and taking care of yourself before you can do the same for others. When you can find peace in uncertainty because forgiveness and trust are moral virtues installed in your heart, you start living in the present and truly show up. The only thing guaranteed in life is death. Only you are responsible for making the time in between birth and death worthwhile.

Stop being your own enemy.

Here is your final journal prompt:

You get to define your own success, so what are you waiting for?

ACKNOWLEDGEMENTS

You just finished reading an entire book filled with my words, yet those words cannot adequately convey the depth of appreciation, and gratitude I hold for the people in my life. Without them, undertaking the journey of writing this novel might not have been possible. The unconditional love, support, and genuine honesty I am blessed with are truly unmatched. I credit the love and value I have deepened within myself to the people closest to me who encouraged this growth.

Thank you to everyone who made the stories and experiences, including the hurt and heartbreak, in this novel possible—I will always hold love for you. To all my family and close friends who continue to make a lasting impact on me daily, you know who you are.

Special thanks to Uncle Mark for believing in me.

Ben, thank you for being the most incredible confidant and my biggest fan throughout this process.

Mom, Dad, and Taylor—you all mean the world to me.

I was forewarned that writing a book would be tough; I didn't expect it to be as challenging as it turned out to be. This has been the most demanding and rewarding experience of my life. Revisiting past experiences to write every single page of this book was draining, yet healing. The encouragement I received throughout this process has been unparalleled. A special thanks to my editor, Lisa Caskey, and mentor, Hussein Al-Baiaty—without your wisdom, guidance, pure kindness, and ability to talk me off multiple ledges, this process wouldn't have been nearly as successful or enjoyable.

I am confident that this book can and will be helpful in someone else's life. For that reason, I am thankful for the people in my life who have now made me thankful for myself for committing to write this book.

ABOUT THE AUTHOR

Kayla Logue graduated from the University of South Carolina Beaufort with a BA in Communications, earning Magna Cum Laude honors. During her time there, her colleague and she founded and hosted the University Broadcast. Her passion for writing ignited during her college years, when she pursued journalism, contributing essays to university publications that faculty recognized as some of the best among submissions. As President of the Communications Club and a participant in the exclusive Chancellor's course for writing and work at the university, she was honored with the Communications Studies Award, the highest departmental recognition.

She then moved to Alexandria, VA, and took on the role of Director of Communications and HR for a small government consulting firm, serving as the subcontractor on Army Logistics Projects. There, Kayla crafted multiple press releases and delivered project updates to Army Generals and Colonels. Seeking a lifestyle change, she transitioned to managing two reformer Pilates studios, Solidcore, where she was responsible for overseeing thirty coaches and held the role of "CEO" of the studios.

Amidst the challenges of 2020, marked by the start of the COVID pandemic and the end of her marriage, Kayla embarked on a new journey. During this period, she managed local social media accounts and laid the foundation for her sister's current full-time business. In February 2021, she joined a land development/real estate company, as a Property Specialist. Within four months, she obtained real estate licenses in four states where the company holds property and became their #1 Top Sales Producer her first full year. Kayla currently contributes to the company as a sales professional and continues to expand her knowledge, maximizing her skills and strengths by crafting deliberate marketing messages and devising strategies for contacting leads and maintaining client relationships.

She recently founded the non-profit organization Move Into Words. This initiative aims to establish a supportive environment advocating for sustainable mental and physical health habits, enabling young professionals to thrive. The non-profit raises awareness about the impact of journaling to empower individuals in search of purpose. While journaling provides confidence for independent healing, growth, and purpose discovery, the non-profit offers a supportive community, so these individuals do not have to navigate their journeys alone.

We are all experts in our own experiences. Kayla's diverse background reflects the importance of continuous learning from everyone we encounter. Her extensive journey, with writing consistently at its core, reinforces the belief that journaling, a practice she embraced in the summer of 2020, can have a monumental impact on self-discovery, growth, healing, defining, and creating success, and building confidence.